Job Interview Quest

MW00657266

Java**Script**
Interview Questions
You'll Most Likely Be Asked

341
Interview Questions

VIBRANT
PUBLISHERS

Java**Script**
Interview Questions
You'll Most Likely Be Asked

ISBN-10: 1-946383-86-4
ISBN-13: 978-1-946383-86-0

Library of Congress Control Number: 2010938816

This publication is designed to provide accurate and authoritative information in regard to the subject matter covered. The author has made every effort in the preparation of this book to ensure the accuracy of the information. However, information in this book is sold without warranty either expressed or implied. The Author or the Publisher will not be liable for any damages caused or alleged to be caused either directly or indirectly by this book.

Vibrant Publishers books are available at special quantity discount for sales promotions, or for use in corporate training programs. For more information please write to **bulkorders@vibrantpublishers.com**

Please email feedback / corrections (technical, grammatical or spelling) to **spellerrors@vibrantpublishers.com**

To access the complete catalogue of Vibrant Publishers, visit **www.vibrantpublishers.com**

Table of Contents

Dear Reader,

Thank you for purchasing **JavaScript Interview Questions You'll Most Likely Be Asked.** We are committed to publishing books that are content-rich, concise and approachable enabling more readers to read and make the fullest use of them. We hope this book provides the most enriching learning experience as you prepare for your interview.

Should you have any questions or suggestions, feel free to email us at **reachus@vibrantpublishers.com**

Thanks again for your purchase. Good luck with your interview!

- Vibrant Publishers Team

JavaScript Interview Questions

Review these typical interview questions and think about how you would answer them. Read the answers listed; you will find best possible answers along with strategies and suggestions.

This page is intentionally left blank

Chapter **1**

Introduction to JavaScript

1: What is JavaScript?

Answer:

JavaScript is a scripting language that adds interactivity to HTML pages.

2: What kind of language does JavaScript provide?

Answer:

JavaScript is an interpreted language that executes scripts without preliminary compilation.

3: Is there any connection between Java and JavaScript?

Answer:

No. They are different in every way and JavaScript is not as powerful and complex as Java.

4: What is the official name of JavaScript and is it supported by all browsers?

Answer:

The official name of JavaScript is ECMA (European Computer Manufacturer's Association) and with it, Internet Explorer 4 and Mozilla Firefox 1.5 fully supported.

5: What does JavaScript do?

Answer:

JavaScript is meant to be an easy scripting language that helps the non-programmers with its simple syntax. JavaScript is smart enough that it can put dynamic text into HTML pages, it can react to events (like when a page has finished downloading), and it can read and write HTML elements, create cookies and so forth.

6: Does prior knowledge of JAVA ease the use of JavaScript?

Answer:

Yes. Being modeled after Java, which in turn is modeled after C++, JavaScript should be easier to familiarize and work with.

7: Is JavaScript case sensitive?

Answer:

Yes. Unlike HTML, JavaScript has to have all variables and function names (etc.) in capital letters.

8: How do you place JavaScript?

Answer:

JavaScript may be inserted into code with the following syntax:

<script type="text/JavaScript">

9: Where do you place JavaScript?

Answer:

JavaScript may be placed in the <head> or <body> section of HTML code, but it is usually a good practice to place it in <head> as to not hinder your code later on.

This page is intentionally left blank

Chapter **2**

Statements, Comments and Variables

10: How do you terminate statements in JavaScript?

Answer:

In JavaScript, statements are terminated by semicolons (;) and although they are not mandatory they are a good practice to pick up.

11: Why are comments used in JavaScript and how are they inserted?

Answer:

Usually comments are added to make the code more readable but they can also be used to explain the code. They are inserted with //

(for single line comments) and /* */ for multiple lines comments.

12: What are variables and how are they inserted?

Answer:

Variables are storing containers used for holding expressions and values. They can have a short letter or a longer name and are inserted with the statement: var. Because the variables are loosely typed, they can hold any type of data.

13: What does a variable of var y=10; and var catname= "Tomcat"; do?

Answer:

With the execution of the above code, we have variables that hold values of 10(for y) and Tomcat (for catname).

Note that the inclusion of text warrants " " being used.

14: How many statements types can we find in JavaScript? Give some examples?

Answer:

The statement types found in JavaScript are: Expression statements, compound, empty and labeled statements.

Example: break, continue, default, do, for, etc.

15: What are conditional statements and how are they implemented in JavaScript?

Answer:

Conditional statements are used to perform and act on different sets of conditions declared by the programmer. They are the following: if statement; if...else statement; if...else if...else statement and the switch statement.

16: How will you determine a variable type in JavaScript?
Answer:

A variable type in JavaScript is determined using Typeof operator. When the object is String, Number, Function, undefined and Boolean, the operator returns the same type. And when the object is null and array, the operator returns "object".

Example:

var count=100;

typeof count; ⟶ (returns "number")

17: What is the difference in evaluating ["8"+5+2] and [8+5+"2"]?
Answer:

In ["8"+5+2],"8" is a String. So anything that trail the string will be changed to string. Hence the result will be"852".

In [8+5+"2"], 8 and 5 are integer, so it gets added up (13).And "2" is treated as String. Hence the concatenation takes place and the result will be "132".

18: Is it possible to assign a string to a floating point variable?
Answer:

Yes. Any variable can be assigned to another data type. For example,

var a1=10.39;

document.write(a1); ⟶ 10.39

a1="hai";

document.write(a1); ──→ hai

19: Will variable redeclaration affect the value of that variable?

Answer:

No. The same value will be retained in the variable.

Example:

var status="cool";

document.write("status"); //cool

var status;

document.write("status"); //cool

status="chill";

document.write("status"); //chill

20: How will you search a matching pattern globally in a string?

Answer:

A matching pattern can be globally searched in a string using "g" modifier in Regular Expression.

Example:

var p1="First_Regular_ Expression_First";

var q1="/First/g";

document.write("Pattern_Match:" + p1.match(q1)); // Pattern_Match:First,First

21: How will you search a particular pattern in a string?

Answer:

A particular pattern in string can be searched using test function.

If the match is found it returns true, else false.

Example:

var my_pattern1=new RegExp("pp");

document.write(my_pattern1.test("Happy_Days")); //true

22: Which property is used to match the pattern at the start of the string?

Answer:

"^" symbol is used for position matching.

Example:

var p1="First_Regular_ Expression_First";

var q1="/First/^";

document.write("Pattern_Match:" + p1.match(q1));
//Pattern_Match:First ⟶ First_Regular

23: Which property is used to match the pattern at the end of the string?

Answer:

"$" symbol is used for end position matching.

Example:

var p1="First_Regular_ Expression_First";

var q1="/First/$";

document.write("Pattern_Match:" + p1.match(q1));
//Pattern_Match:First ⟶ Expression_First

This page is intentionally left blank

Chapter **3**

Operators and Functions

24: What are operators? Which are the most important operators in JavaScript?

Answer:

Operators in JavaScript are used to combine values that form expressions. The most important are: = and +. The first is used to assign values and the second one is used to add values together.

25: Why comparison and logical operators are used?

Answer:

Comparison operators are used to determine if there is a difference between variables, and also their equality, while the logical operators are used to determine the logic of variables.

26: How many types of pop-up boxes does JavaScript have? What are those?

Answer:

JavaScript has three types of pop-up boxes and they are: alert, confirm and prompt.

27: Does creating an alert box prompt the user to respond with OK or Cancel?

Answer:

No. An alert box only gives the user the option of choosing OK to proceed.

28: What are functions in JavaScript and where are they placed?

Answer:

Functions contain code that is executed before an event thus stopping the browser from loading a script when the page opens. Functions can be placed both in the <head> or <body> section, but it is advised to place them in the <head> section.

Chapter **4**

Values, Arrays and Operators

29: What does the keyword null mean in JavaScript?

Answer:

The keyword null is a special value that indicates no value. It is unique from other values and also fully distinct.

30: What does the value undefined mean in JavaScript?

Answer:

Undefined is a special value in JavaScript, it means the variable used in the code does not exist or is not assigned any value or the property does not exist.

31: Do the null and undefined values have the same conversion in Boolean, numeric and string context?

Answer:

No. The undefined value changes into Nan in numeric context and undefined in a string context. They share the same conversion in Boolean.

32: What are Boolean values?

Answer:

Boolean values are datatypes that only have two types of values: true or false; a value of Boolean type only represents the truth: it says if it true or not.

33: Can a Boolean value be converted into numeric context?

Answer:

Yes. If it is converted into numeric context the true value becomes 1 and if it is a false value it becomes a 0.

34: What happens when a number is dropped where a Boolean value is expected to be?

Answer:

The number is converted into a true value, but only if it not equal to 0 or NaN which in turn is converted into a false value.

35: What are objects in JavaScript?

Answer:

Objects are collections of named values that most of the times are referred to as properties of an object.

36: What is an array in JavaScript?

Answer:

An array is a collection of data values which can handle more than one value at a time, the difference being that each data in an array has a number or index.

37: From which version forward has JavaScript stopped using ASCII character set?

Answer:

From v.3 JavaScript started using Unicode character sets: identifiers can now contain letters and digits from the Unicode complete character set.

38: What is the scope of a variable in JavaScript?

Answer:

The scope of a variable is the region in which your program in which it is defined. Thus a global variable has a global scope meaning it is defined everywhere in your JavaScript code. The local variables have a local scope meaning they are defined only in the body section of your code.

39: In the body of the code which variable with the same name has more importance over the other: the local or the global variable?

Answer:

In the body of a function a local variable will always take precedence over a global variable hiding it all together.

40: How many types of undefined variables can we find in JavaScript?

Answer:

There are two kinds of undefined variables: the first is the one that has never been declared and the second is the kind of undefined variable that has been declared but has never had a value assigned to it.

41: What does (==) & (===) operators do in JavaScript?

Answer:

The first (==) is the equality operator and it checks if its two operands are equal. The second (===) is called the identity operator and it checks if two operands are identical by using a strict definition.

42: How many types of operators can we find in JavaScript?

Answer:

There are eight types of operators in JavaScript. These are as follows: operator, arithmetic, equality, relational, string, logical, bitwise and miscellaneous.

43: How many types of comparison operators does JavaScript contain?

Answer:

There are four types of comparison operators in JavaScript. They are: less than (<); greater than (>); less than or equal (<=) and greater than or equal (>=).

44: Can comparison be done on any type of operands?

Answer:

Yes. Operands in JavaScript that are not number or strings are converted.

45: What are logical operators and how are they used in JavaScript?

Answer:

The logical operators perform Boolean algebra and are used mostly with comparison operators to show complex comparisons that involve more than one variable.

46: Does JavaScript contain classes?

Answer:

Yes. Although they do not define the structure of an object like in Java and C++, it does approximate the classes with its constructors and their prototype objects.

47: What is the purpose of an object in JavaScript?

Answer:

An object is an instance of its class. This allows us to have multiple instances of any class.

48: How are classes and objects in JavaScript named and why?

Answer:

Classes are named with an initial capital letter and an object with lowercase letters. This ensures that classes and objects are distinct from each other.

49: What are class properties in JavaScript?

Answer:

Class property is associated with a class itself and not instance of a class. This ensures that no matter how many instances of a class are created only one copy of each class property exists.

50: What are class methods in JavaScript?

Answer:

Class methods are associated with a class rather than an instance of a class, meaning they are invoked by the class itself and not an instance of the class.

51: Do class properties and class methods have a global and local range?

Answer:

No. They are both only global because they do not operate on a particular object.

52: How do JavaScript equality operators compare objects?

Answer:

Equality operators compare objects by reference and not by value, checking to see if both references are to the same object. They do not check to see if two objects have the same property names and values.

53: Are the null and undefined values for the variable same?

Answer:

No. Variables that are declared and not assigned any value will have undefined values whereas the variable that is assigned a null will have null values.

Example:

var qno; ⟶ "undefined value"

var Items=10;

Items=null; ⟶ "null value"

54: What is the difference between "===" and "=="? Give examples.

Answer:

a) "===" returns true - if both the operands are same and are of the same data type

b) "==" checks only for operands - if both are same, returns true

For comparison of operands, JavaScript converts different data type to same type.

Example:

Let p=3

p=='3' //true   p==='3' //false

3=='3' //true   3==='3' //false

P==3 //true   P===3 //true

55: What is the function of delete operator in JavaScript?

Answer:

It deletes

a) an object

Syntax: delete obj_name1;

b) particular element in an array

   Syntax: delete arr_ele1[index];

c) property of an object

   Syntax: delete obj_name2.prop_name;

56: How will you clip the particular portion of an element?

Answer:

Using clip property of the style object, we can clip a particular portion of an element.

Example:

my_obj1.style.clip="values";

my_obj1 ⟶ document object, getElementById property

values ⟶ auto(Unclip),rect(top1,right1,botttom1,left1)-pin the shape defined by value.

Chapter 5

Modules, Characters and Attributes

57: How is a module in JavaScript written so that it can be used by any script or module?

Answer:

The most important rule is to never define global variables as to have the risk of having that value overwritten by a module or another programmer.

58: How are regular expressions represented and created in JavaScript?

Answer:

Regular expressions are represented by the RegExp objects and are created by the RegExp() constructor or a special literal syntax.

59: How do you combine literal characters in JavaScript?

Answer:

Literal characters can be combined into character classes by placing them within square brackets.

60: What document properties does a document contain?

Answer:

In a document we can find the following properties: bgcolor, cookie, domain, lastModified, location, referrer, title and URL.

61: How many types of DOM document object collections can we find in JavaScript?

Answer:

There are five DOM properties that give access to special elements within a document: anchors, applets, forms, images and links.

62: Does use of DOM properties allow you to change the structure of a document?

Answer:

No. Using these properties you can inspect and alter a link and read values from a link but the text in the document cannot be changed; the structure of the document cannot be altered.

63: How are document objects named in JavaScript?

Answer:

Documents are named with the name attribute of forms. You can change elements, links and images when the name attribute is present. Its value is used for exposure to the corresponding object by name.

This page is intentionally left blank

Chapter 6

Event Handlers and DOM

64: How are event handlers defined in JavaScript?

Answer:

Event handlers are defined by assigning a function to an event handler property, unlike HTML where event handlers are defined by giving a string of JavaScript code to an event handler attribute.

65: What do the HTMLInputElement and HTMLFormElementinterfaces define in HTML DOM?

Answer:

The HTMLInputElement defines focus() and blur() methods and form property. HTMLFormElementinterfaces defines submit() and reset() methods and length property.

66: How many levels of DOM standard are currently released?

Answer:

There are two levels of DOM: the first one was released in 1998 and it defines the core DOM interfaces. The second level that was released in 2000 that updates the core interfaces and defines standard APIs for working with document events style sheets CSS.

67: Are there any more levels of DOM?

Answer:

Yes there are. One of them is the level 3 DOM, but its features are not fully supported by all the web browsers and the other is the level0 DOM whish in fact is the legacy DOM.

68: What does the Node interface define in DOM?

Answer:

The node interface defines the childNotes, firstChild, lastChild, nextSibling and previousSibling properties.

69: How do you find document elements in a HTML document?

Answer:

You can find elements by using the getElementsByTagName and obtain any type of HTML element.

70: How are documents created and modified in DOM?

Answer:

Documents are modified by setting attribute values on document elements with the element.setAttribute() method. They are created with document.createDocumentFragment().

71: How can you build a DOM tree of arbitrary document content?

Answer:

You can achieve this by creating new Element and text nodes with the Document.CreateElement() and Document.CreateTextNote() methods; you can then add them to a document with the Note.AppendChild(), Note.InsertBefore() and Note.replaceChild() methods.

72: How do you find document elements in IE4?

Answer:

Because IE4 does not support the getElementById() and get ElementsBytagName()methods we are forced to use the array property named all().

73: How to access Html attributes using DOM?

Answer:

Using three methods of DOM:

a) **getAttribute():** Retrives the value of an attribute
b) **setAttribute():** Modifies the value of an attribute
c) **removeAttribute():** Removes the entire attributes from an element

74: What is the difference between getAttribute() and getAttributeNode()?

Answer:

a) **getAttribute():** returns the value of an attribute

b) **getAttributeNode():** returns the attribute itself

Example:

```
<body>
<p id="ki" attr="Ish">Hellllo</p>
  <script>
    txt1=document.getElementById('ki').getAttribute('attr');
    document.write(txt1 + "<br>");
    txt2=document.getElementById('ki').getAttributeNode('attr');
    document.write(txt2.name +"  :   ");
    document.write(txt2.value);
  </script>
</body>
```

75: What are the event handlers in JavaScript?

Answer:

Event handlers are the JavaScript code that can be used inside the Html tags and gets executed when any events such as form submission, page loading occur. Some of the event handlers in JavaScript are:

a) onload

b) onunload

c) onclick

d) onmouseout

e) onmouseover

76: Can you use two or more functions in onclick event?

Answer:

By separating the functions with semicolon(;) we can use two or more functions. First function gets executed after onclick event. The consecutive functions get executed only when the immediate previous function returns true.

Example:

onclick=("my_fun1();my_fun2();my_fun3()");

This page is intentionally left blank

Chapter **7**

Keywords, CSS and CSS2

77: What is the "this" keyword in JavaScript?

Answer:

When an event handler with an HTML or JavaScript property is defined a function to a property of a document element is assigned. When the event handler is invoked the "this" keyword refers to the target element.

78: What does lexically scoped in JavaScript mean?

Answer:

It means that functions run in the scope that they are defined in and not in the scope they are called in.

79: Is the following expression correct: element.style.font-family= "arial";?

Answer:

No. It is incorrect because in JavaScript many CSS style attributes contain hyphens in their names and these are interpreted as minus signs.

Chapter **8**

Statements and Functions

80: How can you replace an if-else statement in JavaScript?

Answer:

You can simply replace if-else statement by using the ternary operator. These kinds of operators require three operands. The ternary operator can be defined as follows:

(condition) ? val1 :val2.

81: What is a "memoization" method in JavaScript?

Answer:

Memoization is an optimization technique used in JavaScript. Functions may use objects to remember the results of previous operations, in this way avoiding unnecessary work.

82: What does 2+3+"1" evaluate to?

Answer:

As 2 and 3 are integers, 2+3 will evaluate to 5. Since "1" is a string, it will concatenate with 5 and the final result will be the string "51"

Chapter 9

Roles of JavaScript, Scripts and Events

83: Give some examples of the role that JavaScript has on the Web.

Answer:

The role of JavaScript is to provide a better user browsing experience. JavaScript can do many things like: creating visual effects such as image rollovers, sorting the columns of a table, so the user can easily find what he needs and hiding certain content.

84: Give an example on how JavaScript can be used in URLs.

Answer:

JavaScript can be used in URLs, using "JavaScript:"

pseudoprotocol specifier. This specifies that the body of the URL is an arbitrary string of JavaScript code to be run by the JavaScript interpreter. It is treated as a single line of code, and the statements must be separated by semicolons. A JavaScript URL can look like this one:

JavaScript:varJavaScript:varJavaScript:varJavaScript:varJavaScript :varJavaScript:varJavaScript:varJavaScript:varJavaScript:varJavaSc ript:varJavaScript:varJavaScript:varJavaScript:varJavaScript:varJav aScript:varJavaScript:var today = new Date(); "<p>The date is:</p>" + today;

85: How are scripts in JavaScript executed?

Answer:

Scripts are executed in the order in which they appear and the code in the <script> tags is executed as part of document loading process.

86: What do scripts placed in the <head> part of an HTML document do?

Answer:

Scripts placed in the <head> section usually define functions that are to be called by other code and/or declare and initialize variables used by other code.

87: What do scripts placed in the <body> part of an HTML document do?

Answer:

Scripts placed in the <body> part of a document can do everything that those placed in a <head> section of the document do. They can also manipulate document elements that appear before the script.

88: When does browser trigger the onload event?

Answer:

The browser triggers the onload event and executes any registered JavaScript code under the following scenarios:

a)   Once the document has been parsed,

b)   All scripts were executed and

c)   All auxiliary content has finished loading.

For all the major browsers (except IE), the JavaScript onload event does not trigger when the page loads as a result of a Back button operation. Rather the event is triggered only when the page is loaded.

89: When does the onunload event trigger and what does it do?

Answer:

The onunload event triggers after the user navigates away from the web page giving the code on that page a final chance to run; the onunload event enables the possibility to undo effects of your onload handler or scripts in the web page.

90: How can we read or write a file in JavaScript?

Answer:

Client-side JavaScript does not provide any way to read, write or delete files or directories on the client computer. This is also a security aspect – with no File object and no file access functions, a JavaScript program cannot delete a user's data.

91: Explain about "cross-site scripting".

Answer:

Cross Site Scripting (XSS) is called as the name of a security issue where the hacker or attacker injects the scripts or HTML tags into a website.

Even though defending XSS attack is a job for server-side script developers, the JavaScript programmers should also be aware of cross site scripting and defend against this attack.

92: What are JavaScript timers? Give examples and explain one of them.

Answer:

It is very important for any programming environment to have the ability to schedule code to be executed at some point in the future. Client-side JavaScript provides some global functions like: setTimeout(), clearTimeout(), setInterval(), clearInterval(). For example setTimeout() method schedules a function to run after a specific number of milliseconds elapses.

93: Explain the history property in JavaScript?

Answer:

The history property of the Window object refers to the History object for the window. The History object supports three methods: back(), forward() and go(). The first 2 methods are similar with what happens when the user clicks on the Back and Forward browser buttons. The go() method takes an integer argument and can skip any number of pages

94: What is the "Screen" object?

Answer:

The screen property of the Window object refers to a Screen object that provides information about the size of the user's display, the number of colors available on it. The "width" and "height" properties can be used to specify the size of the display in pixels.

95: What is the "Navigator" object?

Answer:

The navigator property of a Window object refers to a Navigator object that contains important information about the web browser, such as the version and the list of data formats it can display. In the past Navigator object was used by scripts to determine if they were running in Internet Explorer or in Netscape web browser.

96: What is "onreset" in JavaScript?

Answer:

Onreset is an event handler of a form object in JavaScript. It gets executed when the reset button in the form is clicked and resets the fields when it receives true value otherwise prevent the form elements from being reset.

Example:

onreset="alert('AABBCC')"

97: What is void 0 in JavaScript?

Answer:

a) JavaScript files can be executed directly in the web browsers by placing "JavaScript:" before the code

b) Web browsers attempt to load the page when any value

returning JavaScript's code is executed

c)   void 0 is used to prevent the unwanted action

98: What is the best practice to place the JavaScript codes?

Answer:

Place all JavaScript codes in one place. So it can be placed,

a)   At the end of html tag

b)   Below second header tag

c)   Before the closing of bod tag

99: How to prevent caching of web pages in temporary internet files folder?

Answer:

Caching of web pages in temporary internet files folder can be prevented by adding <META HTTP-EQUIP="PRAGMA" CONTENT="NO-CACHE" > in the second header tag which is placed before the html's end tag(</html>).

Example:

```
<html>
  < head >
    <META HTTP-EQUIV="REFRESH" CONTENT="3">
  </ head >
  <body>
    <p>Hellllo</p>
  </body>
  < head >
    <META Http-equiv="PRAGMA" Content="NO-CACHE">
```

```
</head>
</ html >
```

100: Why adding of meta tag in first header will not prevent caching of the Web page?

Answer:

The browsing page gets cached only when the buffer is half filled. So when the meta tag is added in first header, the internet explorer search for that page in cache at that instant. Most of the time, buffer won't get half filled at the beginning of parsing.

101: What is the purpose of meta tag?

Answer:

When this tag is read while parsing the html code, internet explorer searches for this page in cache at that instant. If it is found, it will be removed from the cache.

Syntax:

<META Http-equiv="PRAGMA" Content="NO-CACHE">

102: How will you resolve looping problem in JavaScript?

Answer:

Using closures which combines the function with its referencing environment, looping can be resolved. It keeps the local variable of the function alive even after the function returned the value. When there is function within the function, Closure is created.

103: Give any example for resolving looping problem.

Answer:

```
var method1={};
for(var k=0;k<5;k++){
  method1[i]=function(){
    document.write("Iteration:" + k + "< >");
  };
}
for(var m=0;m<5;m++){
  method1[j]();
}
```

Output:

4 4 4 4 4 instead of 0 1 2 3 4

By adding closure,this can be rectified.

```
method1[i]=function(n){
  return function(){
    document.write("Iteration:" + n + "< >");
    }
  })(k);
```

Output:

0 1 2 3 4

104: When is the Execution context created and what are the primary components?

Answer:

During execution of JavaScript function, the execution context is created. It keeps track of the execution of its related code. Global execution context is created when executing the application.

a) **LexicalEnvironment:** Resolves the identifier references

b) **VariableEnvironment:** Records the variable-function declaration bindings

c) **ThisBinding:** value of "this" keyword related with execution context

105: When is the Execution context stack created?

Answer:

a) **Global execution context:** Created when executing the application

b) **New execution context:** Created when the new functions are created

c) **Collection of this execution context form the execution context stack**

106: How is the outer scope environment references maintained?

Answer:

Using LexicalEnvironment, the outer scope environment references are maintained. It contains two components:

a) **Environment Record:** Identifier bindings are stored for the execution context

b) **Outer Refernces:** Points to the declaration of execution context in lexicalEnvironment

107: How will you read or write in a file using JavaScript?

Answer:

An I/O operation such as reading or writing is not possible.

However, "Java Applet" can be implemented to read files for script.

108: How will you create rich, responsive display and editor user interface?

Answer:

Using knockout we can create rich, responsive display and editor user interface. It is JavaScript library which implements the model view-viewmodel pattern. It is used to create UI and allows dynamic updation and can be used with any server or client.

109: Which is the new JavaScript engine developed for internet explorer9 by Microsoft?

Answer:

Chakra is the new JavaScript engine for IE9. A distinct feature is that its JIT compiles scripts on separate "CPUcore", parallel to web browsers. The engine also accesses the computer's graphic processing unit for 3D videos and graphics. To execute scripts on traditional web pages and to improve JavaScript runtime and libraries, a new interpreter was included.

110: What is Node.js?

Answer:

Node.js is a software designed for creating server side JavaScript application which is not executed in client browser. It is event based and runs asynchronously to provide scalability and reduce overhead.

111: Which is alternative to XML for data exchange in JavaScript?

Answer:

JSON (JavaScript Object Notation). Light weighted, text-based data exchange format. Web data is imported into JavaScript applications using JSON.

Example: JSON Object creation

var obj_json1={"Company_name":"ABC","Experiance":"5"};

document.write("Co Name:" + obj_json1.Company_name); //Co Name:ABC

112: What are the sub-components of dynamic component in JavaScript?

Answer:

a) **Dynamic typing:** Based on values; not associated on variable

b) **Obj-based:** Properties of an object can be modified at run-time; Built-in functions are used for properties to maintain dynamicity

c) **Run-time evaluation:** eval() is used for run time evaluation and will take dynamic arguments at run time

This page is intentionally left blank

Chapter **10**

Opening and Manipulating Windows

113: How can you open a new window using JavaScript?

Answer:

We can open a new web browser window using "open()" method of the Window object.Window.open() has four optional arguments and returns a window object that represents the new open window. The first argument is the URL of the document to display in the new window (if it is null or empty string, the window will be empty), the second argument is the name of the window; the third parameter is a list of features that specify the window size and GUI decoration. The fourth argument is useful only when the second argument is mentioned.

114: How can you close a window using JavaScript?

Answer:

We can close a created window object using "close()" method. The syntax is: Window.close()

115: What does the "location" function do in JavaScript?

Answer:

The location property of a window is a reference to a location object and represents the URL of the document that is displayed in the window. The Href property of the location object is a string that contains all the text of the URL.

116: What other properties besides Href can we find in the "location" function in JavaScript?

Answer:

Other properties that we can use are: protocol, host, pathname and search.

117: What happens when a string value is added to the location function in JavaScript?

Answer:

The browser interprets the string as a URL and tries to load it and display the document and that URL.

118: What is the history object in JavaScript?

Answer:

The history object refers to the History of the browser window.

The multitudes of elements that the history object incorporates are never accessible to scripts.

119: Which are the methods supported by the history object in JavaScript?

Answer:

There are three methods supported by the history object: the back(), the forward() and the go().

120: How many and which are the coordinates of a browser within the HTML document?

Answer:

There are three types of coordinates and these are: screen, window and document coordinates.

This page is intentionally left blank

Chapter **11**

Objects and their Properties in JavaScript

121: Name the properties of Navigator in JavaScript.

Answer:

There are five properties for the navigator object and these are: appName, appVersion, userAgent, appCodeName and platform.

122: What happens when confirm() or prompt() methods are used in JavaScript?

Answer:

When these boxes are initialized the code stops running and the currently loading document stops loading until the user response with the requested input.

123: What happens when the mouse is moved over a hyperlink in JavaScript?

Answer:

JavaScript code evaluates the onmouseover attribute and sets the status property of the window, thus returning the "true" value telling the browser not to take any actions.

124: What does the "defaultStatus" property do in JavaScript?

Answer:

The "defaultStatus" property enables text to be displayed in the status line when the browser does not find anything to display. Newer versions of the current browser have this property deprecated.

125: What is the "onerror" property in JavaScript?

Answer:

The "onerror" property has a special status: the function the user assigns becomes an error handler for the window; the function assigned to the property is invoked when an error occurs in that window.

126: What arguments does the error handler receive when an error occurs in JavaScript?

Answer:

The error handler receives three arguments: the first is the message that describes the error; the second is the string that contains the URL of the document containing the JavaScript code that caused the error and the third argument is line number within the document where the error occurred.

127: In addition to the three arguments that the error handler receives, is its return value of any importance?

Answer:

The return value of the error handler is significant: if the onerror handler returns True then the browser does not display its own error message having been told that the handler has taken care of the error.

128: How can JavaScript code refer to a window or frame object?

Answer:

In JavaScript we can refer in any window or frame to its own window or frame using "window" or "self". They are necessary to use when the programmer needs to refer to this global object itself. In case the programmer wants to refer to a method or property of the window/frame, it is not necessary to prefix the property or method name with "window" or "self".

129: What is a DOM (Document Object Model)?

Answer:

DOM (Document Object Model) is an API that defines the way to access the objects that compose a document. W3C defines a standard DOM that is reasonably well supported in all modern browsers.

130: What does the method write() of the Document object do?

Answer:

The write() method allows users to write content into the document. The write() method is part of DOM and it can be used in two ways. First of all, it can be used within a script to output HTML into the document being parsed. Second, write() can be used (in conjunction with open() and close() methods of the Document object) to create entirely new documents in other windows or frames.

131: How will you determine an object type?

Answer:

Using "Instanceof and isprototypeof" by checking its instance and prototype respectively.

Example: document.writeln(book1 instanceof Book);

var Book = function() {...};

Book.prototype.constructor == Book; //return true.

132: What is alert and confirm box in JavaScript?

Answer:

a) Alert and confirm both are pop ups in JavaScript and take the focus of the user from the current page to pop ups

b) Alert provides the user with "ok" button whereas confirm provides with "ok" and "cancel" button where user can select any one of the options

c) When "ok" is selected, confirm returns true else false

133: What are the properties of array object?

Answer:

a) Index property

b) Input property

c) Length property

d) Constructor property

e) Prototype property

134: What are the sub objects of the windows object in JavaScript?

Answer:

a) **Document object:** Work with DOM and provides interface to XML and Html documents and allow CSS manipulations

b) **Frame object:** Represents <frame> HTML frames. Frame object will be created for each <frame> tag

c) **Location object:** Contains the current URL information "window.location"

d) **History object:** Contains the URL history visited by the user

135: What is the use of userAgent of navigator object?

Answer:

a) Identifies the operating system of the client's machine

b) "appVersion" and "userAgent" can also be used

c) "userAgent" property of navigator object returns the value of the user agent header sent by the browser to server

Syntax:

document.write(navigator.userAgent);

document.write(navigator.appVersion);

136: What are the ways to delete the property of an object and

how?

Answer:

It can be deleted in two ways.

Example:

oven=new Object();

oven.name="LG";

oven.color="Black";

    a) using object name and property

         example: delete oven.color;

    b) using object name and property with "with" statement

         example: with(oven)

            delete color;

137: What is the use of eval() in JSON?

Answer:

JSON can be parsed using the built-in function eval() and JSON data is executed to generate native JavaScript object.

Example:

obj_json2=eval('(' + JSON_text+')');

138: What are the advantages of JSON over XML?

Answer:

    a) JSON provides array and object type and also some scalar data types whereas XML does not provide any data types

    b) Formatting is done by direct mapping in JSON whereas it is complex in Xml

    c) Document size is too large in XML. When the data grows,

amount of xml also grows whereas documents are compact in JSON

XML:

```
<Record>
  <First_Name>abcd</First_Name>
  <Age>25</Age>
</Record>
```

JSON:

```
{
"Record":{"First_Name":"abcd","Age":"25"}
}
```

139: How can the properties of JavaScript objects be accessed?

Answer:

The properties of JavaScript objects be accessed in the two ways shown below:

Syntax:

  a) obj_name.prop1;

  b) obj_name["prop1"];

140: What are the objects of navigator objects?

Answer:

  a) **Window object:** gets created for every frame and web browser

  b) **Mime type object:** using enabledplugin, gets information about the plugin

  c) **Plugin object:** gives information about an installed plug-in

141: How to access the properties of main window from the secondary window?

Answer:

This can be done using Opener property. The properties of the main window can be accessed from secondary window.

Example:

In the secondary window:

window.opener.document.bgColor="my_color_value"; //give color name or hex code

It changes the background color of the primary window to the given color.

142: How will you load the previous and next url from the history list?

Answer:

The previous and next url from the history list can be loaded using back and forward function of history object.

Example:

"history.back()";

"history.forward()";

143: How will you determine whether the browser has cookies enabled?

Answer:

The browser status can be determined using cookieEnabled function of navigator object. If cookies are enabled returns true, else false.

Example:

If(navigator.cookieEnabled)

   document.write("Enabled");

else

   document.write("Not Enabled");

This page is intentionally left blank

Chapter **12**

JavaScript and HTML

144: How can you change the font size of an Element in JavaScript? Give an example.

Answer:

document.getElementById(elementId).style.fontSize = "12";

In this case, JavaScript and CSS are very similar, because the CSS style rules are laid on top of the DOM.

145: How can you submit a form using JavaScript?

Answer:

This can be done using document.form[0].submit(), where 0 represent the index of the form in the page. If there are more than one form in the page, then the first form has index 0, the second form has index 1 and so on.

146: How can you set the background color of an HMTL document?

Answer:

This can be easily done using document.bgcolor = "color", where color can be the name of a color – e.g. red, black, or it can represent the code of the color – e.g. #00FF34.

147: Name the Boolean operators in JavaScript.

Answer:

The Boolean operators in JavaScript are: '&&' - AND operator, '||' – OR operator '!' - NOT operator.

148: How can we determine the state of a checkbox in JavaScript?

Answer:

var isChecked = window.document.getElementById(elementId).checked – isChecked is the name of the variable where the true or false value will be stored. ElementId represents the id of the checkbox element. If the checkbox is checked this will return true, otherwise false.

149: How can you create an HTML button and what is the event called when the button is pressed?

Answer:

An HTML button can be created like this: <input type="button"> or <button type="button"> and the event is "onclick"

150: How will you make loading of JavaScript code after Html by the browser?

Answer:

By "defer" script we can load JavaScript code after Html. It informs the browser to load all html codes before JavaScript. So the code inside the defer script gets executed only when the page is entirely parsed. It can use on both external and inline scripts.

Example:

<script type='text/javascript' src='a1.js' defer='defer'></script>

Here loading of a1.js takes place after all html code has been parsed.

151: Which popup allows the user to enter the input?

Answer:

Prompt box allows the user to enter the input. It provides the user with text box for input and two buttons ("ok and cancel"). On selecting "Ok", it returns true otherwise false.

Example:

var a1= prompt("content1","myDefault_val");

152: What are the ways to display the message on screen?

Answer:

   a) Using write method.

       Eg: document.write("hello");

   b) Using getElementById.

       Eg: function disp(text) {

            var m1 = document.getElementById("my_disp");

m1.innerHTML = text;

return true;

}

153: How will you reload the page from server using JavaScript?

Answer:

Using reload() we can reload a page. It is a function of location object that contains the details of present url. It takes either true or false as argument. Default argument is false. When set to false, reloads the page from cache. Otherwise ask the browser to load the page from server.

Syntax:

Window.location.reload(value);

154: How will you display large tables effectively in JavaScript?

Answer:

Using fixed width table we can display large tables effectively. Fixed width tables are provided by the browser based on the width of the columns in the first row, ensuring faster display.

Advantage: No need for the browser to wait till all data is received to infer the best width.

Syntax:

In css,set "table-layout:fixed"

155: How will you create pop window using JavaScript?

Answer:

It can be created as below:

a) **window.open():** opens a new browser window

Syntax:

Window.open(page_Url, window_
name,properties,replace);

For pop window,replace is always set to false.

b) **window.showDialogBox():** creates a modal dialog box

Syntax:

window.showDialogBox(page_url,window_name,properties
);

156: How will you fix the errors that make the JavaScript engines difficult to perform optimization?

Answer:

Using "Strict Mode" which makes the code run faster than the code without strict mode such errors could be fixed. To enable strict mode, insert 'use strict mode' before the code. It takes care of following functions:

a) Duplications are not allowed

b) If Deprecated languages is used, throws error

c) It denounces 'with' statement

d) Assign to read-only variables are not allowed

157: How will you make secure JavaScript code?

Answer:

a) Using Strict Mode. The value passed with the "this" (keyword) to a function will not be changed in strict mode

b) When a function is in strict mode, fn_name.arguments and

fn_name.caller throws error when tried to get or set

158: How will you add the external JavaScript file?

Answer:

External JavaScript file should be saved with an extension ".js" and needs to be imported to the html file by adding that file's path to the "src" attribute of <script> tag.

Example:

<html>

<head>

  <script src="aa.js"></script>

</head>

<body>...</body>

</html>

159: Is it possible to break up a string in a JavaScript code?

Answer:

Yes. Using backslash" \ ", a text can break up in a code.

Example:

document.write("Break \

up a code");

     ⟶ document.write \

("Cannot break like this"); // This is not possible.

160: What is the use of "wait" property in cursor style?

Answer:

Wait sets the cursor in wait state when the request is on process.

Type of cursor can be set or returned by using "cursor property". Some of the type of cursor are:

a) **default:** default cursor

b) **wait:** loading symbol or hourglass

c) **auto:** browser default cursor

d) **help:** arrow with a question mark symbol

Syntax:

myobject.style.cursor="my_value";

eg: myobject-window,document, my_value-wait,auto,help...

161: What are the properties that can be set in the background properties?

Answer:

a) **color:** sets the bgcolor

b) **image:** sets the bgimage

c) **repeat:** repeats the bgimage

d) **attachment:** makes the image fixed or scrolls with the page

e) **position:** sets the starting position of an image

Syntax:

my_object.style.background="my_value";

    // my_object=>window,document,..

    // my_value=>color,image,reappear,attachment,position

162: What are the ways to set the background color?

Answer:

The background color can be set in the following two ways:

a) Using bgColor

my_obj.bgcolor="my_color"

    my_obj ⟶ document

    my_color ⟶ colors,color value

b) Using background

    my_obj.style.backgroundColor="my_value";

      my_obj ⟶ document

      my_value=color,image,reappear,attachment,position

163: How will you add JavaScript files dynamically?

Answer:

By creating a new script element file and append it to the document, we can add JavaScript files dynamically.

Example:

```
var head_elemt=document.getElementByTagName("...."); //pass tag name like"head"
var my_script=document.createElement('...'); //pass type as script
my_script.type='text/javascript';
my_script.src='www.abc.co/ab.js';
head_elemt.appendChild(my_script);
```

164: How will you get the current "x and y" co-ordinate value of the window when it is scrolled?

Answer:

a) Using onscroll. It executes when the window is scrolled

b) pageXOffset and pageYOffset are used to get the co-ordinate value

Example:

window.onscroll=function(){

var xvalue=window.pageXOffset ;

document.write(xvalue);}

165: What are the methods to create remote window?

Answer:

a) **Using custom property**

Secondary window:

windw2=window.open("remote_win2");

windw2.maker=self; //"self" gives the current window

Remote window:

function remote_wind2(link2){

 maker.location=link2;

}

<input type="button" value="Address" onclick=remote_wind2()>

b) **Using opener property**

function remote_windw2(link1){

 window.opener.location=link;

}

<input type="button" value="Address" onclick=remote_windw2()>

166: How will you get the height of the browser window?

Answer:

a) Using availHeight property of the screen object.

b) Gives the height of the browser window excluding the
    taskbar height,etc..

Example:

document.write("Height:" + screen.availHeight);

167: How will you get the language code of the linked page?

Answer:

Using hreflang property of the anchor object we can get the
language code of the linked page. Anchor object creates a link to
another page or document.

Example:

my_anchor_object1.hreflang;

168: How would you input a file?

Answer:

Using FileUpload Object we can input a file. The type should be
specified as "file" in the <input> tag. It creates the fileupload
object that opens the file dialog box on clicking the button.

Example:

<input type="file" >

Chapter **13**

JavaScript Forms

169: What is the importance of the "name" attribute of a <form> tag?

Answer:

When a Form object is created, the name attribute is stored as an element in the form[] array of the Document object, and it is also stored in the properties of the Document objects. So, after defining a <form name="formName">, it will be easy to refer the Form object using document.formName instead of document.form[0]. This attribute has nothing to do with submitting the form.

170: What are the event handlers of the form element?

Answer:

The following event handlers are supported by form elements:

onclick, onchange, onfocus, onblur.

171: What does "onchange" event handler do?

Answer:

This event handler is triggered when the user enters text or selects an option, changing in this way the value represented by the element. Button and other related elements do not support this event handler because they don't have a value that can be edited. This event it is triggered when the focus is lost and it is moved to another form element.

172: What is a "cookie"?

Answer:

A cookie is a named data stored by the web browser and associated with a particular web page or web site. They were originally designed for the server-side programming and they are implemented as an extension to the HTTP protocol. The cookie data is transmitted between the client and the server and the server-side scripts can read and write cookie values that are stored on the client. In JavaScript, cookies are manipulated using "cookie" property of the Document object.

173: What does the "new" operator do?

Answer:

The "new" operator creates a new object, that has no properties, and then it invokes the function passing the new objected created as the value of "this" keyword. The function that uses the "new" operator is called "constructor function" or just simply "constructor".

174: What does <optgroup> tag do in JavaScript?

Answer:

It is used with select statement to group the related options in the drop down list. It will be useful to display long list.

Example:

<select>

  <optgroup label="JAVA">

<option value="hibernate1">Hibernate</option>

<option value="struts1"> Struts </option>

  </optgroup>

  <optgroup label="WEBSERVICE">

    <option value="soap1">SOAP</option>

    <option value="xml1"> Xml </option>

  </optgroup>

</select>

175: Compare between session state and view state.

Answer:

Functions	Session State	View State
Maintenance	Session level-data of user sessions	Page level maintenance-state of page
Visibility	State value available to all pages within the user's session	State value of one page is not visible to another page
Storage	State information stored in server	State information stored in client
Data	Permanently store the user specific data in server	Permanently store the page instance specific data in client

176: Which function is better for fast execution: window.onload or window.onDocumentReady?

Answer:

window.onDocumentReady is better for fast execution because it executes the code once DOM is loaded by the browser and will not wait for the object such as images to be loaded whereas onLoad executes only when the browser loads DOM and all other resources such as images gets loaded.

177: What is the purpose of "visibility" property in JavaScript?

Answer:

a) **"Visibility":** Makes the element either visible or invisible

b) **"collapse":** Used to hide the elements in a table

c) **"inherit":** Takes the values from the parent element

Example:

my_elemt.style.visibility="my_val";

my_val ⟶ visible,hidden,collapse,inherit

178: What are the ways to make an element visible/hidden?

Answer:

a) **Using display property**

my_elemt.style.display=" "; //visible

my_elemt.style.display="none"; //hidden

b) **Using visibility property**

my_elemt.style.visibility="visible"; //visible

my_elemt.style.visibility="hidden"; //hidden

179: How will you disable the html form fields, for instance password field?

Answer:

Using disabled property of a password object.

Example:

document.getElementById("Field_Id").disabled=true;

180: How will you select the contents in the text field, say password?

Answer:

Using select function of password object, we can select the contents in text field.

Example:

document.getElementById("Field_Id").select();

181: How will you display the id of the form and the name attribute of the hidden element?

Answer:

Using "form" and name property of hidden object, we can display the id of the form and the name attribute of the hidden element

Example:

var form_id1=
document.getElementById("my_elemt_id").form.id;

var name_id2= document.getElementById("my_elemt_id").name;

182: How will you get the last row from a table in JavaScript?

Answer:

Using tFoot property of a table object we can get the last row from a table. The last rows of tables in Html can be combined using the tfoot element.

Example:

my_table_objects.tFoot;

my_table_objects ⟶ document object,getElementById property

183: How will you create and delete caption to a table?

Answer:

Using createCaption and deleteCaption function of the table object.

Example:

my_table_objects.createCaption(); //create

my_table_objects.deleteCaption(); //delete

my_table_objects ⟶ document object,getElementById property

184: How will you create a text area and make it read-only?

Answer:

a) **Using textarea object**

Example:

<textarea id="my_txt" cols="22">

My_text

</textarea>

b) **Using readOnly property of textarea object**

Example:

my_table_objects.readOnly="my_value1"; //delete

my_table_objects ⟶ document object,getElementById
property

my_value1 ⟶ true

185: How will you change the caption display position of a table?

Answer:

Using captionSide property of the style object we can change the caption display position of a table.

Example:

my_obj1.style.captionSide="values";

my_obj1 ⟶ document object,getElementById property

values ⟶ top/bottom

This page is intentionally left blank

Chapter **14**

JavaScript Constructors

186: What does a JavaScript constructor do?

Answer:

The constructor initializes the newly created object and sets any properties that need to be set before that object is used. You can easily define a constructor function, by writing a function that adds properties to "this" operator.

Example:

```
// define the constructor
function circle(r){
this.radius = r;
}
//invoke the constructor to create a circle object:
```

var circle1 = new circle(3); // we pass the radius value to the constructor so that it will initialize the new object appropriately.

187 What is the value that the constructor function returns?

Answer:

Typically, the constructor does not return any values. They simply initialize the object passed as the value of "this" operator and return nothing. Anyway, the constructor can return an object value, but in this case the returned object becomes the value of the "new" expression and the object that was the value of this is simply not taken into account.

188: How many types of common object methods can we find in JavaScript?

Answer:

We have three types of object methods: the toString I () method; the valueOf() method and comparison method.

189: How does class hierarchy manifest themselves in JavaScript?

Answer:

Java and C++ have an explicit concept of the class hierarchy; so any class can be extended or sub-classed so that subclass that results can be inherited. JavaScript supports prototype inheritance instead of class-based inheritance so the Object class is the most generic with all other classes as specialized versions of it or subclasses.

190: What does "overriding method" mean?

Answer:

If a subclass defines a method that has the same name as the method in the superclass it is called overriding that method. This is a common thing to do when creating subclasses of existing classes. For example when toString() method is defined, the toString() method of Object is overridden.

191: How can you create an XML document in Firefox using JavaScript?

Answer:

We can create an empty XML Document in Firefox and related browsers with document.implementation.createDocument() which is a DOM Level 2 method.

192: How are images accessed from JavaScript?

Answer:

Images can be referred using document.images[0] // for the first images, document.images[1] and so one for the next images. Once the image is accessed, you can perform different tasks on them.

193: Where is the arguments() array placed in JavaScript?

Answer:

It is placed and defined only within a function body. Within the arguments of a body arguments refers to Arguments object for the function.

194: Which are the properties of the arguments object in

JavaScript?

Answer:

The properties of the arguments object are callee and length. All values that are passed as arguments become array elements of the arguments object.

195: What happens when a function is invoked with the arguments object?

Answer:

Arguments object is created for it and the local variable arguments are initialized to refer that arguments object.

Chapter 15

Miscellaneous Arguments, Functions and Methods in JavaScript

196: What does arguments.callee do in JavaScript?

Answer:

The arguments.callee refers to the currently running function and it provides a way for an unnamed function to refer to itself.

197: What does arguments.length do in JavaScript?

Answer:

The arguments.length specifies the number of arguments that are passed to the current function; it only specifies the number of arguments actually passed and not the expected number.

198: What other JavaScript method you know that is similar with shift() method?

Answer:

Other method similar with shift() is Array.pop(), the only exception is that it operates on the beginning of an array rather that the end.

199: How can you remove a page from the browser history?

Answer:

If the programmer wants to remove the current page from the browser history, it can simply use location.replace() method. Invoking this method causes the browser to request a page through a GET method just like a regular web page.

200: How can you pass data between pages using cookies?

Answer:

In this case cookies.js library can be used with onunload event handler of one page to store 1 to 20 name/value pairs on the user's machine. In the second document, the onload event handler is used to retrieve the cookie data and assign the value to a text input field with the same name located on the second page.

201: What is the difference between resizeTo() and resizeBy() methods?

Answer:

Both the given methods are applicable to window object. In case you want to resize the window to a specific pixel size, resizeTo() method is the most appropriate. To increase or decrease the size of the window by a fixed pixel amount, you can use resizeBy() method.

202: What is the difference between moveTo() and moveBy() methods?

Answer:

Both the methods are applicable to window object. The first method, moveTo() is used to move the window to a screen coordinate point, by the other hand, the moveby() method shifts the position of the window by a known pixel amount.

203: How can a window that is buried beneath other windows be brought back to the front?

Answer:

In this case, for any window to which you have a valid reference, the focus() method must be invoked.

204: What happens when a string argument is passed with the Date() constructor in JavaScript?

Answer:

If one string argument passes with the Date() constructor it results in the string being a representation of a date in the format that is accepted by the Date.parse() method.

205 Which are the arguments of the Date() constructor in JavaScript?

Answer:

The date() constructor arguments are: milliseconds1, datestring, year, month, day, hours, minutes, seconds and milliseconds2 (optional argument).

206: What does URIError indicate in JavaScript?

Answer:

The URIError indicates that one or more escape sequences in URI are malformed and they cannot be correctly sequenced.

207: What does the encodeURIComponent function do in JavaScript?

Answer:

It is a global function that returns an encoded copy of the string argument.

208: What does the string argument do in JavaScript?

Answer:

The string argument is a string that simply contains a portion of a URI or other text that has to be encoded.

209: What is and what does the escape() function do in JavaScript?

Answer:

The escape() function is a global function that returns a new string that contains an encoded version of s; the string s by itself is not modified.

210: What does the apply() function do in JavaScript and which are its arguments?

Answer:

The apply() function invokes the specified function and treats it like it were a method of thisobj argument passing it then the arguments contained by the args array.

211: What does the getClass() function do in JavaScript?

Answer:

The getClass() function takes a JavaObject object as an argument and return the JavaClass object of the respective JavaObject.

212: What is Infinity in JavaScript?

Answer:

Infinity is a global property that contains special numeric value that represents positive infinity; it cannot be deleted by the delete operator.

213: What does the exec() method do in JavaScript?

Answer:

The exec() is the most powerful pattern-matching method of RegExp and String. It searches string for text that matches the regexp and if it finds a match returns an array of results; if not it returns null.

214: What happens when the exec() method is invoked on a nonglobal pattern?

Answer:

The exec() performs a search and then returns the same result as String.match() would.

215: Does exec() include full details of every match even if regexp is not global?

Answer:

It is different in this regard to String.match() which return less information when used with global patterns.

216: What is an anchor in JavaScript?

Answer:

An anchor is a named location within an Html document that is created with an <a> tag that has an attribute specified.

217: What does the focus() method do in JavaScript?

Answer:

The focus() method scrolls the document so that the anchor location is visible; it is created by any standard HTML <a> tag that contains a name attribute.

218: Is JSObject a JavaScript object?

Answer:

No. JSObject is a Java class that cannot be used in any JavaScript programs; it invokes the JavaScript methods into Java.

219: What does the call() method of JSObject class do?

Answer:

It invokes a name method of the JavaScript object represented by the JSObject; the arguments are passed to the method as an array of Java objects, then the return value of the JavaScript method is returned as a Java object.

220: What does the eval() method of the JSObject do?

Answer:

It evaluates the JavaScript code that is contained within a string s in the context of the JavaScript object. Its behavior is similar to that of the eval() method of JavaScript.

221: What does the getSlot() method of the JSObject do?

Answer:

It reads and returns the value of an array element that is specified at the index of a JavaScript object.

222: What does the removeMember() method of the JSObject do?

Answer:

It deletes a named property that belongs to the JavaScript object represented by the JSObject.

223: What does the setMember() method of the JSObject do?

Answer:

This method is the opposite of removeMember in that it sets a value of a named property of a JavaScript object from Java.

224: What does the toString() method of JSObject do?

Answer:

It invokes the toString() of the JavaScript object and returns the result of that method.

225: What does the (n) argument represent in isFinite(n) and what does it return?

Answer:

The (n) argument is the number that is to be tested and if n can be converted or is a finite number return true and false or NaN if n is positive or negative infinity.

226: What does the isNaN() function do in JavaScript?

Answer:

It tests its arguments to see if it is the value of Nan, which is an illegal number.

227: What does the setYear() function do in JavaScript?

Answer:

It sets the year field of a specified date object with a special behavior for years between 1900 and 1999.

228: What does the join() method do in JavaScript?

Answer:

Put in all the elements of the array into a string separed by the specified separator. Default separartor is comma ",".

Example:

var fourwheelers = ["Car","Bus","Lorry"] ;

document.write(fourwheelers.join("-")); ⟶ "Car-Bus-Lorry"

229: How will you pop the last element from an existing array?

Answer:

Using pop() function we can pop the last element from an existing array. It removes and returns the last element of an array. Length of the array will decrease by 1.

Example:

var no=[1,2,3];

document.write(no); ⟶ "1,2,3"

document.write.(no.pop() +"<br>"); ⟶ "3"

document.write(no); ⟶ "1,2"

230: How to pop the first element from an existing array?

Answer:

Using shift() function we can pop the first element from an existing array. It removes and returns the first element of an array. Length of the array will decrease by 1.

Example:

var no=[1,2,3];

document.write(no); ⟶ "1,2,3"

document.write.(no.shift() +"<br>"); ⟶ "1"

document.write(no); ⟶ "2,3"

231: How will you add one or more elements to the end of the existing array?

Answer:

Using push() function we can add more elements. It adds the new items to the end of the array and returns its length.

Example:

var no=[1,2,3];

document.write(no); ⟶ "1,2,3"

document.write(no.push(5)); ⟶ "4"

document.write(no); ⟶ "1,2,3,5"

232: How will you add one or more elements to the beginning of the existing array?

Answer:

Using unshift() function we can add more elements. It adds the new items to the begining of the array and returns its length.

Example:

var no=[1,2,3];

document.write(no); ⟶ "1,2,3"

document.write(no. unshift (5)); ⟶ "4"

document.write(no); ⟶ "5,1,2,3"

233: How will you reverse the elements in an array?

Answer:

Using reverse() function without creating new array.

Example:

var no=[1,2,3];

document.write(no); ⟶ "1,2,3"

document.write(no.reverse()); ⟶ "3,2,1"

234: What does the Array.slice(start,end) method do in JavaScript and how to retrieve the elements within the selected position in an array?

Answer:

Its returns the array object containing the elements starting from the specified start value till the element before the end value. When a negative value is used for the start or end values, that gets added to the length of the array and returns the elements within that position.

235: What does the Array.sort() method do in JavaScript?

Answer:

a) **Default sort():** used to sort the alphabets in ascending order

b) **reverse() is used with the sort():** Used to sort the alphabets in descending order

c) **To sort the numbers,** some functions are passed as arguments in sort()

236: What is encodeURI( ) and encodeURIComponent( )?

Answer:

a) Used to encode the given uri

b) encodeURI() encodes the special characters except " : @ $ # = & / + ? "

c) encodeURIComponent encodes all the special characters including " : @ $ # = & / + ? "

237: What is decodeURI( ) and decodeURIComponent( )?

Answer:

a) Used to decode the given encoded uri. decodeURI() decodes the special characters except " : @ $ # = & / + ? "

b) decodeURIComponent denotes all the special characters including " : @ $ # = & / + ? "

238: What does the splice( ) function do in JavaScript?

Answer:

Adds or remove elements to/from an existing array and return the removed elements.

array.splice(index,no of items to be removed,new items1,new items2...new itemn);

Example:

var no=[1,2,3,4,5];

document.write(no); ⟶ "1,2,3,4,5"

document.write(no. splice (1,2,9,10)); ⟶ "2,3"

document.write(no); ⟶ "1,9,10,4,5"

239: How will you print the current window using JavaScript?

Answer:

Using window.print() function to print the contents of the specified window.

240: How will you get default value when an argument is not passed in calling function?

Answer:

By Shorthand assignment. It checks whether the passed argument contains a value.

Example:

```
function add1(a1,a2){
    var b1=a1 || 1; ⎯⎯▶ b1=5
    var b2=a2 || 2; ⎯⎯▶ b2=2
    return b1+b2; ⎯⎯▶ 7
}
add1(5);
```

Here, since the first argument is only passed, it is treated as true hence"5" gets assigned to b1. Since the Second argument is not passed, it is treated as undefined value (i.e.) false hence the default value gets assigned.

241: How will you encode and decode a string?

Answer:

a) **Using escape() and unescape()**

b) **escape():** Encodes the string and special characters except " + * - _ . @ / " . It converts the non Ascii codes to two or four digit hex format

c) **unescape():** decodes the encoded string

242: How will you pass a function as argument to another function?

Answer:

Using callback. A function that is passed as a argument to another function gets a reference called "Callback". The callback functions gets executed only after the execution of called function.

Example:

```
function  oven(time,callback){
  document.write("Started at" +time+ "<br>");
  callback();
}
oven(5,function(){
  document.write("Stopped");});
```

Output:

Started at 5

Stopped

243: What is the need for callback function?

Answer:

When a function is called, execution of the function takes place which will return some value. If the execution time will be longer for the function to return a value, for instance, when it may have to wait for some input from another function or user, it needs to be implemented asynchronously using callback function.

244: How will you get a substring from a string in JavaScript?

Answer:

a) **substring():** Retrieves the string starting from the start value till end value. White space are included

Syntax: substring(start_value,end_value);

b) **substr():** Retrieves the string starting from the start value till the length specified

Syntax: substr(start_value,leng);

Example:

var a="color my world";

document.write(substring(3,7);   // r my

document.write(substr(3,7);   // o my wo

245: How will you get the function (fn1) which recently called the current function (fn2)?

Answer:

Using "fn2.caller" we can get the fn1 info. If the control of the program is in the fn2(), it will return the function (fn1) by which fn2 is recently called by using fn2.caller.

"fn2.arguments" gives the arguments passed to the fn2.

Example:

```
function fn_2(){
    use strict mode;
    fn_2.caller;
    fn_2.arguments;
}
function fn_1(){
fn_2();
}
```

246: How will you execute the page that is about to be unloaded, before the execution of onload()?

Answer:

Using onbeforeunload we can execute the page that is about to be unloaded. The "onunload" function occurs when the page is closed or navigating to another page. Hence onbeforeunload alerts the user about navigation before "onunload".

Example:

```
window.onbeforeunload=alert_msg();
function alert_msg(){
    return "Message to be displayed to the user.";
}
```

247: How will you find whether the window is closed or not?

Answer:

Using closed property we can check the status of the window. It returns "true" if the window is closed else returns "false".

Example:

```
if(window.opener.closed)
    document.write("closed");
else
    document.write("open");
```

248: How will you call a function repeatedly for a particular interval of time?

Answer:

Using setInterval function we can repeatedly call a function for a period of time.. It also clears the timer by returning unique id which will be passed as a parameter for clearTimer.

Example:

```
setInterval(my_funct_1(),444);
```

my_funct_1 ⟶ function to be called

444 ⟶ specified_ interval

249: What is the difference between test and exec function?

Answer:

a) Both functions are used to search the particular pattern.

b) test function returns a Boolean value and exec function returns the found value.

This page is intentionally left blank

Chapter **16**

JavaScript Design Patterns

250: What is a Pattern and explain about design patterns in software programming?

Answer:

A Pattern is often a theme of recurring objects or events. It could be a model or template that could be used to develop or generate a working component. In software development, a pattern is a solution to a common problem. A pattern is more of a best practice or a template which could be used to solve various categories of problems.

Design pattern is a reusable architecture or program that could be reused during the development of any software which usually speed up the development activity. Reusing the Design Patterns always helps to prevent subtle issues which could cause major concerns. Reusing design patterns also improves code readability for architects and coders.

251: Why is it important to identify patterns?
Answer:

Identifying patterns is very important because:

a) Patterns always help us to write better code with proven best practices. There is no need to reinvent the wheel.

b) Patterns always provide an abstraction level – When you build a more complex problem, patterns helps not to think of the low-level details but by default includes the low-level details with self-contained blocks.

c) Patterns often improves the communication between software developers and their teams even when they don't communicate face to face.

252: What is Singleton Pattern and what is its importance in JavaScript?
Answer:

When the number of instances for a particular object is limited to just one, then that single instance is called the Singleton.

Following are the importance of Singleton:

a) Singletons are particularly useful when system-wide actions are needed to be coordinated from one single location. For example: consider database connection pool. The database connection pool often manages creation, destruction, and ensures that the database connections are never lost for the entire application.

b) Singletons mainly reduces the need for the global variables.

In JavaScript, global variables are important because it limits the variable name collisions and namespace pollution.

253: How will you create singleton in JavaScript?
Answer:

We can create Singleton by creating a simple object using the object literal. For Example:

```
var mySingletonObj = {
   myProp: 'My Value'
};
```

In the above code snippet,

mySingletonObj is the simple object created and

myProp: 'My Value' is the object literal.

254: How will you create 2 equal objects in JavaScript?
Answer:

We could create 2 equal objects with the help of new keyword. For example:

```
var myObject1 = new Mars();
var myObject2 = new Mars();
myObject1 === myObject2 //This returns true
```

In the above code snippet, myObject1 is created only the first time when the constructor Mars is called. The second time (and third, fourth, and so on) the same myObject1 object is returned. This is why myObject1 === myObject2 — since they are mainly two references that are pointing to the same exact object.

255: What is the purpose of Factory pattern?

Answer:

The Factory Pattern similar to other patterns is also used to create objects. But here are the two main purposes:

a) Perform repeating operations while setting up similar objects

b) Create objects without actually knowing the specific object type during compile time

256: How will you create a Factory pattern?
Answer:

In JavaScript, Factory pattern could be created as follows:

```
var myCorolla = MakeCar.factory('Compact');

var myIkon = MakeCar.factory('SUV');
```

In the above code snippet, we have a method that accepts a string at runtime and then creates and returns objects of the requested type. There are no constructors used with new or any object literals, but just a function that creates objects based on a type identified by a string.

257: Explain about Iterator pattern.
Answer:

In Iterator pattern, the object holds aggregate data. The data could be stored in a complex structure, and we have to provide access to each element. The object consumer does not need to know the data structure.

For Example:

```
var myElement;
while (myElement = myData.next()) {
  console.log(myElement);
```

}

In the above code, myData has collection of data and each element of them could be accessed by simply calling the next() method in a loop.

258: Explain about Decorator Pattern.

Answer:

In Decorator pattern, a new or additional functionality could be added to an object dynamically during runtime. Objects are mutable in JavaScript, so adding a functionality to an object could be done quite easily.

The main feature of the decorator pattern is configuration and customization of the existing object.

```
var mySale = new Sale(1000); // the price is 1000 Rupees

mySale = mySale.decorate('tax'); // add tax

mySale.getModifiedPrice(); // "Rs1012.88"
```

In the above code, we decorate the code (add additional functionality) with a tax for the mySale object and then get the modified price.

259: What is the importance of Strategy Pattern?

Answer:

The strategy pattern enables you to select algorithms at runtime. The clients of your code can work with the same interface but pick from a number of available algorithms to handle their specific task.

For example, consider the problem of solving form validation using strategy pattern. You can create one validator object with a validate() method. This is the method that will be called regardless of the concrete type of form and will always return the same result. The result will be list of data that didn't validate and return any error messages.

260: Explain data validation using strategy pattern.

Answer:

Let's say you have the following piece of data, probably coming from a form on a page, and you want to verify whether it's valid:

```
var myData = {
    firstName: "Spider",
    lastName: "Man",
    myAge: "UnKnown",
    userName: "spider_man"
};
```

We need to configure the validator first and set the rules of what you consider to be valid and acceptable. Let's say we accept anything for first name, the age should be a number and the username to have letters and numbers and no special characters. The configuration will be something like:

```
validator.config = {
    firstName: 'isNonEmpty',
    myAge: 'isNumber',
    userName: 'isAlphaNum'
};
```

Now that the validator object is configured to handle data, we call the validate() method and print any validation errors to the console:

```
validator.validate(myData);
```

```
if (validator.hasErrors()) {

  console.log(validator.messages.join("\n"));

}
```

This could print the following error messages:

Invalid value for *age*, the value can only be a valid number, e.g. 1, 3 10, etc.,

Invalid value for *username*, the value can only contain characters and numbers, and no special symbols

261: Explain Facade pattern with example.
Answer:

The facade is a simple pattern; it provides an alternative interface to an object. It's a good design practice to keep the methods short and not have them handle too much work.

For example, when handling browser events, we have the following methods:

```
stopPropagation(); //Traps the event and doesn't let it bubble up
to the parent nodes

preventDefault();  //Doesn't let the browser do the default action
(for example, following a link or submitting a form)
```

The above are two different methods with unique purpose, but the above two methods are often called together at the same time. So rather than duplicating the above two method calls all over the application, we could create a façade method and that invokes both the methods.

```
var myEvent = {

  stop: function (e) {

    e.preventDefault();
```

```
    e.stopPropagation();
  }
};
```

In the above code, myEvent is a Façade that invokes 2 methods when it's triggered.

262: Explain about Proxy Pattern.

Answer:

In Proxy design pattern, one object acts as an interface to the other object. The proxy sits in the middle of the object and the client object to protect access to the object.

Proxy pattern may look like an overhead but it's useful to improve the performance. The proxy serves as a guardian of the object and tries to have the real subject do as little work as possible.

Network request is one of the expensive operation you could perform in web application. Proxy pattern is useful to make this expensive operation and it's necessary to combine HTTP requests as often as possible.

263: Explain about Mediator pattern.
Answer:

Irrespective of the applications are small or large, applications are made of unique objects. All these unique objects need a way to communicate among themselves in a manner that doesn't affect maintenance and the ability to safely change a part of the application without breaking the rest of it. This is where Mediator pattern plays an important role.

When the application grows, we add objects one by one and it grows rapidly. Then, during refactoring, objects are removed and rearranged. When objects know too much about each other and communicate directly by calling each other's methods and change the properties, it leads to undesirable tight coupling.

When objects are closely coupled, it's not easy to change one object without affecting many others. Then even the simplest change in an application is no longer trivial, and it's virtually impossible to estimate the time a change might take. The mediator pattern alleviates this situation by promoting loose coupling and helping to improve maintainability.

264 Explain about Observer Pattern.
Answer:

The *Observer* pattern is mainly used in client-side JavaScript programming. All the browser events like key-press, mouse-over, and so on are examples of Observer pattern.

Another name for this pattern is *custom events* since they were created programmatically as opposed to the ones that the browser triggers.

This pattern is also called as *subscriber / publisher* pattern. The main motivation for this pattern is to promote loose coupling. Instead of one object calling another object's method, an object subscribes to another object's specific activity and gets notified.

The subscriber is also called as observer. The object being observed is called as subject or publisher. The publisher calls or notifies all the subscribers when an event occurs and this pass a message in the form of an event object.

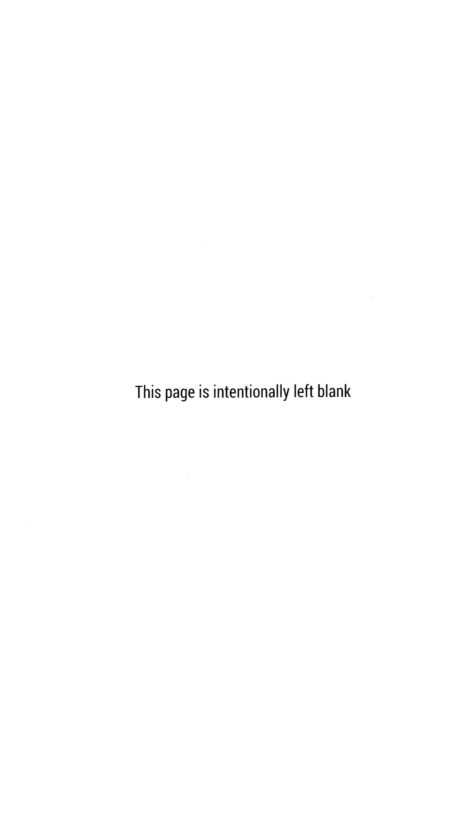

This page is intentionally left blank

HR Interview Questions

Review these typical interview questions and think about how you would answer them. Read the answers listed; you will find best possible answers along with strategies and suggestions

1: Tell me about a time when you worked additional hours to finish a project.

Answer:

It's important for your employer to see that you are dedicated to your work, and willing to put in extra hours when required or when a job calls for it. However, be careful when explaining why you were called to work additional hours – for instance, did you have to stay late because you set goals poorly earlier in the process? Or on a more positive note, were you working additional hours because a client requested for a deadline to be moved up on short notice? Stress your competence and willingness to give 110% every time.

2: Tell me about a time when your performance exceeded the duties and requirements of your job.

Answer:

If you're a great candidate for the position, this should be an easy question to answer – choose a time when you truly went above and beyond the call of duty, and put in additional work or voluntarily took on new responsib-ilities. Remain humble, and express gratitude for the learning opportunity, as well as confidence in your ability to give a repeat performance.

3: What is your driving attitude about work?

Answer:

There are many possible good answers to this question, and the interviewer primarily wants to see that you have a great passion for the job and that you will remain motivated in your career if hired. Some specific driving forces behind your success may include hard work, opportunity, growth potential, or success.

4: Do you take work home with you?

Answer:

It is important to first clarify that you are always willing to take work home when necessary, but you want to emphasize as well that it has not been an issue for you in the past. Highlight skills such as time management, goal-setting, and multi-tasking, which can all ensure that work is completed at work.

5: Describe a typical work day to me.

Answer:

There are several important components in your typical work day, and an interviewer may derive meaning from any or all of them, as well as from your ability to systematically lead him or her through the day. Start at the beginning of your day and proceed chronologically, making sure to emphasize steady productivity, time for review, goal-setting, and prioritizing, as well as some additional time to account for unexpected things that may arise.

6: Tell me about a time when you went out of your way at your previous job.

Answer:

Here it is best to use a specific example of the situation that required you to go out of your way, what your specific position would have required that you did, and how you went above that. Use concrete details, and be sure to include the results, as well as reflection on what you learned in the process.

7: Are you open to receiving feedback and criticisms on your job performance, and adjusting as necessary?

Answer:

This question has a pretty clear answer – yes – but you'll need to display a knowledge as to why this is important. Receiving feedback and criticism is one thing, but the most important part of that process is to then implement it into your daily work. Keep a good attitude, and express that you always appreciate constructive feedback.

8: What inspires you?

Answer:

You may find inspiration in nature, reading success stories, or mastering a difficult task, but it's important that your inspiration is positively-based and that you're able to listen and tune into it when it appears. Keep this answer generally based in the professional world, but where applicable, it may stretch a bit into creative exercises in your personal life that, in turn, help you in achieving career objectives.

9: How do you inspire others?

Answer:

This may be a difficult question, as it is often hard to discern the effects of inspiration in others. Instead of offering a specific example of a time when you inspired someone, focus on general principles such as leading by example that you employ in your professional life. If possible, relate this to a quality that someone who inspired you possessed, and discuss the way you have modified or modeled it in your own work.

10: What has been your biggest success?

Answer:

Your biggest success should be something that was especially meaningful to you, and that you can talk about passionately – your interviewer will be able to see this. Always have an answer prepared for this question, and be sure to explain how you achieved success, as well as what you learned from the experience.

11: What motivates you?

Answer:

It's best to focus on a key aspect of your work that you can target as a "driving force" behind your everyday work. Whether it's customer service, making a difference, or the chance to further your skills and gain experience, it's important that the interviewer can see the passion you hold for your career and the dedication you have to the position.

12: What do you do when you lose motivation?

Answer:

The best candidates will answer that they rarely lose motivation, because they already employ strategies to keep themselves inspired, and because they remain dedicated to their objectives. Additionally, you may impress the interviewer by explaining that you are motivated by achieving goals and advancing, so small successes are always a great way to regain momentum.

13: What do you like to do in your free time?

Answer:

What you do answer here is not nearly as important as what you don't answer – your interviewer does not want to hear that you like to drink, party, or revel in the nightlife. Instead, choose a few activities to focus on that are greater signs of stability and maturity, and that will not detract from your ability to show up to work and be productive, such as reading, cooking, or photography. This is also a great opportunity to show your interviewer that you are a well-rounded, interesting, and dynamic personality that they would be happy to hire.

14: What sets you apart from other workers?

Answer:

This question is a great opportunity to highlight the specific skill sets and passion you bring to the company that no one else can. If you can't outline exactly what sets you apart from other workers, how will the interviewer see it? Be prepared with a thorough outline of what you will bring to the table, in order to help the company achieve their goals.

15: Why are you the best candidate for that position?

Answer:

Have a brief response prepared in advance for this question, as this is another very common theme in interviews (variations of the question include: "Why should I hire you, above Candidate B?" and "What can you bring to our company that Candidate B cannot?"). Make sure that your statement does not sound rehearsed, and highlight your most unique qualities that show the interviewer why he or she must hire you above all the other candidates. Include specific details about your experience and special projects or recognition you've received that set you apart, and show your greatest passion, commitment, and enthusiasm for the position.

16: What does it take to be successful?

Answer:

Hard work, passion, motivation, and a dedication to learning – these are all potential answers to the ambiguous concept of success. It doesn't matter so much which of these values you choose as the primary means to success, or if you choose a combination of them. It is, however, absolutely key that whichever value you choose, you must clearly display in your attitude, experience, and goals.

17: What would be the biggest challenge in this position for you?

Answer:

Keep this answer positive, and remain focused on the opportunities for growth and learning that the position can provide. Be sure that no matter what the challenge is, it's obvious that you're ready and enthusiastic to tackle it, and that you have a full awareness of what it will take to get the job done.

18: Would you describe yourself as an introvert or an extrovert?

Answer:

There are beneficial qualities to each of these, and your answer may depend on what type of work you're involved in. However, a successful leader may be an introvert or extrovert, and similarly, solid team members may also be either. The important aspect of this question is to have the level of self-awareness required to accurately describe yourself.

19: What are some positive character traits that you don't possess?

Answer:

If an interviewer asks you a tough question about your weaknesses, or lack of positive traits, it's best to keep your answer light-hearted and simple – for instance, express your great confidence in your own abilities, followed by a (rather humble) admittance that you could occasionally do to be more humble.

20: What is the greatest lesson you've ever learned?

Answer:

While this is a very broad question, the interviewer will be more interested in hearing what kind of emphasis you place on this value. Your greatest lesson may tie in with something a mentor, parent, or professor once told you, or you may have gleaned it from a book written by a leading expert in your field. Regardless of what the lesson is, it is most important that you can offer an example of how you've incorporated it into your life.

21: Have you ever been in a situation where one of your strengths became a weakness in an alternate setting?

Answer:

It's important to show an awareness of yourself by having an answer for this question, but you want to make sure that the weakness is relatively minor, and that it would still remain a strength in most settings. For instance, you may be an avid reader who reads anything and everything you can find, but reading billboards while driving to work may be a dangerous idea.

22: Who has been the most influential person in your life?

Answer:

Give a specific example (and name) to the person who has influenced your life greatly, and offer a relevant anecdote about a meaningful exchange the two of you shared. It's great if their influence relates to your professional life, but this particular question opens up the possibility to discuss inspiration in your personal life as well. The interviewer wants to see that you're able to make strong connections with other individuals, and to work under the guiding influence of another person.

23: Do you consider yourself to be a "detailed" or "big picture" type of person?

Answer:

Both of these are great qualities, and it's best if you can incorporate each into your answer. Choose one as your primary type, and relate it to experience or specific items from your resume. Then, explain how the other type fits into your work as well.

24: What is your greatest fear?

Answer:

Disclosing your greatest fear openly and without embarrassment is a great way to show your confidence to an employer. Choose a fear that you are clearly doing work to combat, such as a fear of failure that will seem impossible to the interviewer for someone

such as yourself, with such clear goals and actions plans outlined.
As tempting as it may be to stick with an easy answer such as
spiders, stay away from these, as they don't really tell the
interviewer anything about yourself that's relevant.

25: What sort of challenges do you enjoy?

Answer:

The challenges you enjoy should demonstrate some sort of
initiative or growth potential on your part, and should also be in
line with your career objectives. Employers will evaluate
consistency here, as they analyze critically how the challenges you
look forward to are related to your ultimate goals.

26: Tell me about a time you were embarrassed. How did you handle it?

Answer:

No one wants to bring up times they were embarrassed in a job
interview, and it's probably best to avoid an anecdote here.
However, don't shy away from offering a brief synopsis, followed
by a display of your ability to laugh it off. Show the interviewer
that it was not an event that impacted you significantly.

27: What is your greatest weakness?

Answer:

This is another one of the most popular questions asked in job
interviews, so you should be prepared with an answer already.
Try to come up with a weakness that you have that can actually be
a strength in an alternate setting – such as, "I'm very detail-
oriented and like to ensure that things are done correctly, so I

sometimes have difficulty in delegating tasks to others."
However, don't try to mask obvious weaknesses – if you have
little practical experience in the field, mention that you're looking
forward to great opportunities to further your knowledge.

28: What are the three best adjectives to describe you in a work setting?

Answer:

While these three adjectives probably already appear somewhere
on your resume, don't be afraid to use them again in order to
highlight your best qualities. This is a chance for you to sell
yourself to the interviewer, and to point out traits you possess that
other candidates do not. Use the most specific and accurate words
you can think of, and elaborate shortly on how you embody each.

29: What are the three best adjectives to describe you in your personal life?

Answer:

Ideally, the three adjectives that describe you in your personal life
should be similar to the adjectives that describe you in your
professional life. Employers appreciate consistency, and while
they may be understanding of you having an alternate personality
outside of the office, it's best if you employ similar principles in
your actions both on and off the clock.

30: What type of worker are you?

Answer:

This is an opportunity for you to highlight some of your greatest
assets. Characterize some of your talents such as dedicated, self-

motivated, detail-oriented, passionate, hard-working, analytical, or customer service focused. Stay away from your weaker qualities here, and remain on the target of all the wonderful things that you can bring to the company.

31: Tell me about your happiest day at work.

Answer:

Your happiest day at work should include one of your greatest professional successes, and how it made you feel. Stay focused on what you accomplished, and be sure to elaborate on how rewarding or satisfying the achievement was for you.

32: Tell me about your worst day at work.

Answer:

It may have been the worst day ever because of all the mistakes you made, or because you'd just had a huge argument with your best friend, but make sure to keep this answer professionally focused. Try to use an example in which something uncontrollable happened in the workplace (such as an important member of a team quit unexpectedly, which ruined your team's meeting with a client), and focus on the frustration of not being in control of the situation. Keep this answer brief, and be sure to end with a reflection on what you learned from the day.

33: What are you passionate about?

Answer:

Keep this answer professionally-focused where possible, but it may also be appropriate to discuss personal issues you are passionate about as well (such as the environment or volunteering at a soup kitchen). Stick to issues that are non-controversial, and allow your passion to shine through as you explain what inspires you about the topic and how you stay actively engaged in it. Additionally, if you choose a personal passion, make sure it is one that does not detract from your availability to work or to be productive.

34: What is the piece of criticism you receive most often?

Answer:

An honest, candid answer to this question can greatly impress an interviewer (when, of course, it is coupled with an explanation of what you're doing to improve), but make sure the criticism is something minimal or unrelated to your career.

35: What type of work environment do you succeed the most in?

Answer:

Be sure to research the company and the specific position before heading into the interview. Tailor your response to fit the job you'd be working in, and explain why you enjoy that type of environment over others. However, it's also extremely important to be adaptable, so remain flexible to other environments as well.

36: Are you an emotional person?

Answer:

It's best to focus on your positive emotions – passion, happiness, motivations – and to stay away from other extreme emotions that may cause you to appear unbalanced. While you want to display your excitement for the job, be sure to remain level-headed and cool at all times, so that the interviewer knows you're not the type of person who lets emotions take you over and get in the way of your work.

37: How do you make decisions?

Answer:

This is a great opportunity for you to wow your interviewer with your decisiveness, confidence, and organizational skills. Make sure that you outline a process for decision-making, and that you stress the importance of weighing your options, as well as in trusting intuition. If you answer this question skillfully and with ease, your interviewer will trust in your capability as a worker.

38: What are the most difficult decisions for you to make?

Answer:

Explain your relationship to decision-making, and a general synopsis of the process you take in making choices. If there is a particular type of decision that you often struggle with, such as those that involve other people, make sure to explain why that type of decision is tough for you, and how you are currently engaged in improving your skills.

39: When making a tough decision, how do you gather information?

Answer:

If you're making a tough choice, it's best to gather information from as many sources as possible. Lead the interviewer through your process of taking information from people in different areas, starting first with advice from experts in your field, feedback from coworkers or other clients, and by looking analytically at your own past experiences.

40: Tell me about a decision you made that did not turn out well.

Answer:

Honesty and transparency are great values that your interviewer will appreciate – outline the choice you made, why you made it, the results of your poor decision – and finally (and most importantly!) what you learned from the decision. Give the interviewer reason to trust that you wouldn't make a decision like that again in the future.

41: Are you able to make decisions quickly?

Answer:

You may be able to make decisions quickly, but be sure to communicate your skill in making sound, thorough decisions as well. Discuss the importance of making a decision quickly, and how you do so, as well as the necessity for each decision to first be well-informed.

42: Tell me about your favorite book or newspaper.

Answer:

The interviewer will look at your answer to this question in order to determine your ability to analyze and review critically. Additionally, try to choose something that is on a topic related to your field or that embodies a theme important to your work, and be able to explain how it relates. Stay away from controversial subject matter, such as politics or religion.

43: If you could be rich or famous, which would you choose?

Answer:

This question speaks to your ability to think creatively, but your answer may also give great insight to your character. If you answer rich, your interviewer may interpret that you are self-confident and don't seek approval from others, and that you like to be rewarded for your work. If you choose famous, your interviewer may gather that you like to be well-known and to deal with people, and to have the platform to deliver your message to others. Either way, it's important to back up your answer with sound reasoning.

44: If you could trade places with anyone for a week, who would it be and why?

Answer:

This question is largely designed to test your ability to think on your feet, and to come up with a reasonable answer to an outside the box question. Whoever you choose, explain your answer in a logical manner, and offer specific professional reasons that led you to choose the individual.

45: What would you say if I told you that just from glancing over your resume, I can already see three spelling mistakes?

Answer:

Clearly, your resume should be absolutely spotless – and you should be confident that it is. If your interviewer tries to make you second-guess yourself here, remain calm and poised and assert with a polite smile that you would be quite surprised as you are positive that your resume is error-free.

46: Tell me about your worldview.

Answer:

This question is designed to offer insight into your personality, so be aware of how the interviewer will interpret your answer. Speak openly and directly, and try to incorporate your own job skills into your outlook on life. For example, discuss your beliefs on the ways that hard work and dedication can always bring success, or in how learning new things is one of life's greatest gifts. It's okay to expand into general life principles here, but try to keep your thoughts related to the professional field as well.

47: What is the biggest mistake someone could make in an interview?

Answer:

The biggest mistake that could be made in an interview is to be caught off guard! Make sure that you don't commit whatever you answer here, and additionally be prepared for all questions. Other common mistakes include asking too early in the hiring process about job benefits, not having questions prepared when the interviewer asks if you have questions, arriving late, dressing casually or sloppily, or showing ignorance of the position.

48: If you won the $50m lottery, what would you do with the money?

Answer:

While a question such as this may seem out of place in a job interview, it's important to display your creative thinking and your ability to think on the spot. It's also helpful if you choose something admirable, yet believable, to do with the money such as donate the first seventy percent to a charitable cause, and divide the remainder among gifts for friends, family, and of course, yourself.

49: Is there ever a time when honesty isn't appropriate in the workplace?

Answer:

This may be a difficult question, but the only time that honesty isn't appropriate in the workplace is perhaps when you're feeling anger or another emotion that is best kept to yourself. If this is the case, explain simply that it is best to put some thoughts aside, and clarify that the process of keeping some thoughts quiet is often enough to smooth over any unsettled emotions, thus eliminating the problem.

50: If you could travel anywhere in the world, where would it be?

Answer:

This question is meant to allow you to be creative – so go ahead and stretch your thoughts to come up with a unique answer. However, be sure to keep your answer professionally-minded. For example, choose somewhere rich with culture or that would expose you to a new experience, rather than going on an expensive cruise through the Bahamas.

51: What would I find in your refrigerator right now?

Answer:

An interviewer may ask a creative question such as this in order to discern your ability to answer unexpected questions calmly, or, to try to gain some insight into your personality. For example, candidates with a refrigerator full of junk food or take-out may be more likely to be under stress or have health issues, while a candidate with a balanced refrigerator full of nutritious staples may be more likely to lead a balanced mental life, as well.

52: If you could play any sport professionally, what would it be and what aspect draws you to it?

Answer:

Even if you don't know much about professional sports, this question might be a great opportunity to highlight some of your greatest professional working skills. For example, you may choose to play professional basketball, because you admire the teamwork and coordination that goes into creating a solid play. Or, you may choose to play professional tennis, because you consider yourself to be a go-getter with a solid work ethic and great dedication to perfecting your craft. Explain your choice simply to the interviewer without elaborating on drawn-out sports metaphors, and be sure to point out specific areas or skills in which you excel.

53: Who were the presidential and vice-presidential candidates in the recent elections?

Answer:

This question, plain and simple, is intended as a gauge of your intelligence and awareness. If you miss this question, you may well fail the interview. Offer your response with a polite smile, because you understand that there are some individuals who probably miss this question.

54: Explain X task in a few short sentences as you would to a second-grader.

Answer:

An interviewer may ask you to break down a normal job task that you would complete in a manner that a child could understand, in part to test your knowledge of the task's inner workings – but in larger part, to test your ability to explain a process in simple, basic terms. While you and your coworkers may be able to converse using highly technical language, being able to simplify a process is an important skill for any employee to have.

55: If you could compare yourself to any animal, what would it be?

Answer:

Many interviewers ask this question, and it's not to determine which character traits you think you embody – instead, the interviewer wants to see that you can think outside the box, and that you're able to reason your way through any situation. Regardless of what animal you answer, be sure that you provide a thorough reason for your choice.

56: Who is your hero?

Answer:

Your hero may be your mother or father, an old professor, someone successful in your field, or perhaps even Wonder Woman – but keep your reasoning for your choice professional, and be prepared to offer a logical train of thought. Choose someone who embodies values that are important in your chosen career field, and answer the question with a smile and sense of passion.

57: Who would play you in the movie about your life?

Answer:

As with many creative questions that challenge an interviewee to think outside the box, the answer to this question is not as important as how you answer it. Choose a professional, and relatively non-controversial actor or actress, and then be prepared to offer specific reasoning for your choice, employing important skills or traits you possess.

58: Name five people, alive or dead, that would be at your ideal dinner party.

Answer:

Smile and sound excited at the opportunity to think outside the box when asked this question, even if it seems to come from left field. Choose dynamic, inspiring individuals who you could truly learn from, and explain what each of them would have to offer to the conversation. Don't forget to include yourself, and to talk about what you would bring to the conversation as well!

59: What is customer service?

Answer:

Customer service can be many things – and the most important consideration in this question is that you have a creative answer. Demonstrate your ability to think outside the box by offering a confident answer that goes past a basic definition, and that shows you have truly considered your own individual view of what it means to take care of your customers. The thoughtful consideration you hold for customers will speak for itself.

60: Tell me about a time when you went out of your way for a customer.

Answer:

It's important that you offer an example of a time you truly went out of your way – be careful not to confuse something that felt like a big effort on your part, with something your employer would expect you to do anyway. Offer an example of the customer's problems, what you did to solve it, and the way the customer responded after you took care of the situation.

61: How do you gain confidence from customers?

Answer:

This is a very open-ended question that allows you to show your customer service skills to the interviewer. There are many possible answers, and it is best to choose something that you've had great experience with, such as "by handling situations with transparency," "offering rewards," or "focusing on great communication." Offer specific examples of successes you've had.

62: Tell me about a time when a customer was upset or agitated – how did you handle the situation?

Answer:

Similarly to handling a dispute with another employee, the most important part to answering this question is to first set up the scenario, offer a step-by-step guide to your particular conflict resolution style, and end by describing the way the conflict was resolved. Be sure that in answering questions about your own conflict resolution style, that you emphasize the importance of open communication and understanding from both parties, as well as a willingness to reach a compromise or other solution.

63: When can you make an exception for a customer?

Answer:

Exceptions for customers can generally be made when in accordance with company policy or when directed by a supervisor. Display an understanding of the types of situations in which an exception should be considered, such as when a customer has endured a particular hardship, had a complication with an order, or at a request.

64: What would you do in a situation where you were needed by both a customer and your boss?

Answer:

While both your customer and your boss have different needs of you and are very important to your success as a worker, it is always best to try to attend to your customer first – however, the key is explaining to your boss why you are needed urgently by the customer, and then to assure your boss that you will attend to his or her needs as soon as possible (unless it's absolutely an urgent matter).

65: What is the most important aspect of customer service?

Answer:

While many people would simply state that customer satisfaction is the most important aspect of customer service, it's important to be able to elaborate on other important techniques in customer service situations. Explain why customer service is such a key part of business, and be sure to expand on the aspect that you deem to be the most important in a way that is reasoned and well-thought out.

66: Is it best to create low or high expectations for a customer?

Answer:

You may answer this question either way (after, of course, determining that the company does not have a clear opinion on the matter). However, no matter which way you answer the question, you must display a thorough thought process, and very clear reasoning for the option you chose. Offer pros and cons of each, and include the ultimate point that tips the scale in favor of your chosen answer.

67: Why would your skills be a good match with X objective of our company?

Answer:

If you've researched the company before the interview, answering this question should be no problem. Determine several of the company's main objectives, and explain how specific skills that you have are conducive to them. Also, think about ways that your experience and skills can translate to helping the company expand upon these objectives, and to reach further goals. If your old company had a similar objective, give a specific example of how you helped the company to meet it.

68: What do you think this job entails?

Answer:

Make sure you've researched the position well before heading into the interview. Read any and all job descriptions you can find (at best, directly from the employer's website or job posting), and make note of key duties, responsibilities, and experience required. Few things are less impressive to an interviewer than a candidate who has no idea what sort of job they're actually being interviewed for.

69: Is there anything else about the job or company you'd like to know?

Answer:

If you have learned about the company beforehand, this is a great opportunity to show that you put in the effort to study before the interview. Ask questions about the company's mission in relation to current industry trends, and engage the interviewer in interesting, relevant conversation. Additionally, clear up anything else you need to know about the specific position before leaving – so that if the interviewer calls with an offer, you'll be prepared to answer.

70: Are you the best candidate for this position?

Answer:

Yes! Offer specific details about what makes you qualified for this position, and be sure to discuss (and show) your unbridled passion and enthusiasm for the new opportunity, the job, and the company.

71: How did you prepare for this interview?

Answer:

The key part of this question is to make sure that you have prepared! Be sure that you've researched the company, their objectives, and their services prior to the interview, and know as much about the specific position as you possibly can. It's also helpful to learn about the company's history and key players in the current organization.

72: If you were hired here, what would you do on your first day?
Answer:

While many people will answer this question in a boring fashion, going through the standard first day procedures, this question is actually a great chance for you to show the interviewer why you will make a great hire. In addition to things like going through training or orientation, emphasize how much you would enjoy meeting your supervisors and coworkers, or how you would spend a lot of the day asking questions and taking in all of your new surroundings.

73: Have you viewed our company's website?
Answer:

Clearly, you should have viewed the company's website and done some preliminary research on them before coming to the interview. If for some reason you did not, do not say that you did, as the interviewer may reveal you by asking a specific question about it. If you did look at the company's website, this is an appropriate time to bring up something you saw there that was of particular interest to you, or a value that you especially supported.

74: How does X experience on your resume relate to this position?

Answer:

Many applicants will have some bit of experience on their resume that does not clearly translate to the specific job in question. However, be prepared to be asked about this type of seemingly-irrelevant experience, and have a response prepared that takes into account similar skill sets or training that the two may share.

75: Why do you want this position?

Answer:

Keep this answer focused positively on aspects of this specific job that will allow you to further your skills, offer new experience, or that will be an opportunity for you to do something that you particularly enjoy. Don't tell the interviewer that you've been looking for a job for a long time, or that the pay is very appealing, or you will appear unmotivated and opportunistic.

76: How is your background relevant to this position?

Answer:

Ideally, this should be obvious from your resume. However, in instances where your experience is more loosely-related to the position, make sure that you've researched the job and company well before the interview. That way, you can intelligently relate the experience and skills that you do have, to similar skills that would be needed in the new position. Explain specifically how your skills will translate, and use words to describe your background such as "preparation" and "learning." Your prospective position should be described as an "opportunity" and a chance for "growth and development."

77: How do you feel about X mission of our company?

Answer:

It's important to have researched the company prior to the interview – and if you've done so, this question won't catch you off guard. The best answer is one that is simple, to the point, and shows knowledge of the mission at hand. Offer a few short statements as to why you believe in the mission's importance, and note that you would be interested in the chance to work with a company that supports it.

INDEX

JavaScript Interview Questions

Introduction to JavaScript

1:   What is JavaScript and what does it do?

2:   What kind of language does JavaScript provide?

3:   Is there any connection between Java and JavaScript?

4:   What is the official name of JavaScript and is it supported by all browsers?

5:   What does JavaScript do?

6:   Does prior knowledge of JAVA ease the use of JavaScript?

7:   Is JavaScript case sensitive?

8:   How do you place JavaScript?

9:   Where do you place JavaScript?

Statements, Comments and Variables

10:   How do you terminate statements in JavaScript?

11:   Why are comments used in JavaScript and how are they inserted?

12:   What are variables and how are they inserted?

13:   What does a variable of var y=10; and var catname= "Tomcat"; do?

14:   How many statements types can we find in JavaScript? Give some examples?

15:   What are conditional statements and how are they implemented in JavaScript?

16:   How will you determine a variable type in JavaScript?

17:   What is the difference in evaluating ["8"+5+2] and [8+5+"2"]?

18:   Is it possible to assign a string to a floating point variable?

19:   Will variable redeclaration affect the value of that variable?

20:   How will you search a matching pattern globally in a string?

21:   How will you search a particular pattern in a string?

22:   Which property is used to match the pattern at the start of the string?

23:   Which property is used to match the pattern at the end of the string?

Operators and Functions

24:   What are operators? Which are the most important operators in JavaScript?

25:   Why comparison and logical operators are used?

26:   How many types of pop-up boxes does JavaScript have? What are those?

27:   Does creating an alert box prompt the user to respond with OK or Cancel?

28:   What are functions in JavaScript and where are they placed?

Values, Arrays and Operators

29:   What does the keyword null mean in JavaScript?

30:   What does the value undefined mean in JavaScript?

31:   Do the null and undefined values have the same conversion in Boolean, numeric and string context?

32:   What are Boolean values?

33:   Can a Boolean value be converted into numeric context?

34:   What happens when a number is dropped where a Boolean value is expected to be?

35:   What are objects in JavaScript?

36:   What is an array in JavaScript?

37:   From which version forward has JavaScript stopped using ASCII character set?

38:   What is the scope of a variable in JavaScript?

39:   In the body of the code which variable with the same name has more importance over the other: the local or the global variable?

40:   How many types of undefined variables can we find in JavaScript?

41:   What are the (==) (===) and what do they do in JavaScript?

42:   How many types of operators can we find in JavaScript?

43:   How many types of comparison operators does JavaScript contain?

44:   Can comparison be done on any type of operands?

45:   What are logical operators and how are they used in JavaScript?

46:   Does JavaScript contain classes?

47:   What is an object in JavaScript?

48:   How are classes and objects in JavaScript named and why?

49:   What are class properties in JavaScript?

50:   What are class methods in JavaScript?

51:   Do class properties and class methods have a global and local range?

52:   How do JavaScript equality operators compare objects?

53:   Are the null and undefined values for the variable same?

54:   What is the difference between "===" and "=="?

55:   What is the function of delete operator in JavaScript?

56:   How will you clip the particular portion of an element?

Modules, Characters and Attributes

57:   How is a module in JavaScript written so that it can be used by any script or module?

58:   How are regular expressions represented and created in JavaScript?

59:   How do you combine literal characters in JavaScript?

60:   What document properties does a document contain?

61:   How many types of DOM document object collections can we find in JavaScript?

62:   Does use of DOM properties allow you to change the structure of a document?

63:   How are document objects named in JavaScript?

Event Handlers and DOM

64:   How are event handlers defined in JavaScript?

65:   What do the HTMLInputElement and HTMLFormElementinterfaces define in HTML DOM?

66: How many levels of DOM standard are currently released?

67: Are there any more levels of DOM?

68: What does the Node interface define in DOM?

69: How do you find document elements in a HTML document?

70: How are documents created and modified in DOM?

71: How can you build a DOM tree of arbitrary document content?

72: How do you find document elements in IE4?

73: How to access Html attributes using DOM?

74: What is the difference between getAttribute() and getAttributeNode()?

75: What are the event handlers in JavaScript?

76: Can you use two or more functions in onclick event?

Keywords, CSS and CSS2

77: What is the "this" keyword in JavaScript?

78: What does lexically scoped in JavaScript mean?

79: Is the following expression correct: element.style.font-family= "arial";?

Statements and Functions

80: How can you replace an if-else statement in JavaScript?

81: What is a "memoization" method in JavaScript?

82: What does 2+3+"1" evaluate to?

Roles of JavaScript, Scripts and Events

83: Give some examples of the role that JavaScript has on the Web.

84: Give an example on how JavaScript can be used in URLs.

85: How are scripts in JavaScript executed?

86: What do scripts placed in the <head> part of an HTML document do?

87: What do scripts placed in the <body> part of an HTML document do?

88:   When does browser trigger the onload event?

89:   When does the onunload event trigger and what does it do?

90:   How can we read or write a file in JavaScript?

91:   Explain about "cross-site scripting".

92:   What are JavaScript timers? Give examples and explain one of them.

93:   Explain the history property in JavaScript?

94:   What is the "Screen" object?

95:   What is the "Navigator" object?

96:   What is "onreset" in JavaScript?

97:   What is void 0 in JavaScript?

98:   What is the best practice to place the JavaScript codes?

99:   How to prevent caching of web pages in temporary internet files folder?

100: Why adding of meta tag in first header will not prevent caching of the Web page?

101: What is the purpose of meta tag?

102: How will you resolve looping problem in JavaScript?

103: Give any example for resolving looping problem.

104: When is the Execution context created and what are the primary components?

105: When is the Execution context stack created?

106: How is the outer scope environment references maintained?

107: How will you read or write in a file using JavaScript?

108: How will you create rich, responsive display and editor user interface?

109: Which is the new JavaScript engine developed for internet explorer9 by Microsoft?

110: What is Node.js?

111: Which is alternative to XML for data exchange in JavaScript?

112: What are the sub-components of dynamic component in JavaScript?

Opening and Manipulating Windows

113: How can you open a new window using JavaScript?

114: How can you close a window using JavaScript?

115: What does the "location" function do in JavaScript?

116: What other properties besides Href can we find in the "location" function in JavaScript?

117: What happens when a string value is added to the location function in JavaScript?

118: What is the history object in JavaScript?

119: Which are the methods supported by the history object in JavaScript?

120: How many and which are the coordinates of a browser within the HTML document?

Objects and their Properties in JavaScript

121: Name the properties of Navigator in JavaScript.

122: What happens when confirm() or prompt() methods are used in JavaScript?

123: What happens when the mouse is moved over a hyperlink in JavaScript?

124: What does the "defaultStatus" property do in JavaScript?

125: What is the "onerror" property in JavaScript?

126: What arguments does the error handler receive when an error occurs in JavaScript?

127: In addition to the three arguments that the error handler receives, is its return value of any importance?

128: How can JavaScript code refer to a window or frame object?

129: What is a DOM (Document Object Model)?

130: What does the method write() of the Document object do?

131: How will you determine an object type?

132: What is alert and confirm box in JavaScript?

133: What are the properties of array object?

134: What are the sub objects of the windows object in JavaScript?

135: What is the use of userAgent of navigator object?

136: What are the ways to delete the property of an object and how?

137: What is the use of eval() in JSON?

138: What are the advantages of JSON over XML?

139: How can the properties of JavaScript objects be accessed?

140: What are the objects of navigator objects?

141: How to access the properties of main window from the secondary window?

142: How will you load the previous and next url from the history list?

143: How will you determine whether the browser has cookies enabled?

JavaScript and HTML

144: How can you change the font size of an Element in JavaScript? Give an example.

145: How can you submit a form using JavaScript?

146: How can you set the background color of an HMTL document?

147: Name the Boolean operators in JavaScript.

148: How can we determine the state of a checkbox in JavaScript?

149: How can you create an HTML button and what is the event called when the button is pressed?

150: How will you make loading of JavaScript code after Html by the browser?

151: Which popup allows the user to enter the input?

152: What are the ways to display the message on screen?

153: How will you reload the page from server using JavaScript?

154: How will you display large tables effectively in JavaScript?

155: How will you create pop window using JavaScript?

156: How will you fix the errors that make the JavaScript engines difficult to perform optimization?

157: How will you make secure JavaScript code?

158: How will you add the external JavaScript file?

159: Is it possible to break up a string in a JavaScript code?

160: What is the use of "wait" property in cursor style?

161: What are the properties that can be set in the background properties?

162: What are the ways to set the background color?

163: How will you add JavaScript files dynamically?

164: How will you get the current "x and y" co-ordinate value of the window when it is scrolled?

165: What are the methods to create remote window?

166: How will you get the height of the browser window?

167: How will you get the language code of the linked page?

168: How would you input a file?

JavaScript Forms

169: What is the importance of the "name" attribute of a <form> tag?

170: What are the event handlers of the form element?

171: What does "onchange" event handler do?

172: What is a "cookie"?

173: What does the "new" operator do?

174: What does <optgroup> tag do in JavaScript?

175: Comparison between session state and view state.

176: Which function is best for fast execution: window.onload or onDocumentReady?

177: What is the purpose of "visibility" property in JavaScript?

178: What are the ways to make an element visible/hidden?

179: How will you disable the html form fields, for instance password field?

180: How will you select the contents in the text field, say password?

181: How will you display the id of the form and the name attribute of the hidden element?

182: How will you get the last row from a table in JavaScript?

183: How will you create and delete caption to a table?

184: How will you create a text area and make it read-only?

185: How will you change the caption display position of a table?

JavaScript Constructors

186: What does a JavaScript constructor do?

187: What is the value that the constructor function returns?

188: How many types of common object methods can we find in JavaScript?

189: How does class hierarchy manifest themselves in JavaScript?

190: What does "overriding method" mean?

191: How can you create an XML document in Firefox using JavaScript?

192: How are images accessed from JavaScript?

193: Where is the arguments() array placed in JavaScript?

194: Which are the properties of the arguments object in JavaScript?

195: What happens when a function is invoked with the arguments object?

Miscellaneous Arguments, Functions and Methods in JavaScript

196: What does arguments.callee do in JavaScript?

197: What does arguments.length do in JavaScript?

198: What other JavaScript method you know that is similar with shift() method?

199: How can you remove a page from the browser history?

200: How can you pass data between pages using cookies?

201: What is the difference between resizeTo() and resizeBy() methods?

202: What's the difference between moveTo() and moveBy() methods?

203: How can a window that is buried beneath other windows be brought back to the front?

204: What happens when a string argument is passed with the Date() constructor in JavaScript?

205: Which are the arguments of the Date() constructor in JavaScript?

206: What does URIError indicate in JavaScript?

207: What does the encodeURIComponent function do in JavaScript?

208: What does the string argument do in JavaScript?

209: What is and what does the escape() function do in JavaScript?

210: What does the apply() function do in JavaScript and which are its arguments?

211: What does the getClass() function do in JavaScript?

212: What is Infinity in JavaScript?

213: What does the exec() method do in JavaScript?

214: What happens when the exec() method is invoked on a nonglobal pattern?

215: Does exec() include full details of every match even if regexp is not global?

216: What is an anchor in JavaScript?

217: What does the focus() method do in JavaScript?

218: Is JSObject a JavaScript object?

219: What does the call() method of JSObject class do?

220: What does the eval() method of the JSObject do?

221: What does the getSlot() method of the JSObject do?

222: What does the removeMember() method of the JSObject do?

223: What does the setMember() method of the JSObject do?

224: What does the toString() method of JSObject do?

225: What does the (n) argument represent in isFinite(n) and what does it return?

226: What does the isNaN() function do in JavaScript?

227: What does the setYear() function do in JavaScript?

228: What does the join() method do in JavaScript?

229: How will you pop the last element from an existing array?

230: How to pop the first element from an existing array?

231: How will you add one or more elements to the end of the existing array?

232: How will you add one or more elements to the beginning of the existing array?

233: How will you reverse the elements in an array?

234: What does the Array.slice(start,end) method do in JavaScript and how to retrieve the elements within the selected position in an array?

235: What does the Array.sort() method do in JavaScript?

236: What is encodeURI( ) and encodeURIComponent( )?

237: What is decodeURI( ) and decodeURIComponent( )?

238: What does the splice( ) function do in JavaScript?

239: How will you print the current window using JavaScript?

240: How will you get default value when an argument is not passed in calling function?

241: How will you encode and decode a string?

242: How will you pass a function as argument to another function?

243: What is the need for callback function?

244: How will you get a substring from a string in JavaScript?

245: How will you get the function (fn1) which recently called the current function (fn2)?

246: How will you execute the page that is about to be unloaded, before the execution of onload()?

247: How will you find whether the window is closed or not?

248: How will you call a function repeatedly for a particular interval of time?

249: What is the difference between test and exec function?

JavaScript Design Patterns

250: What is a Pattern and explain about design patterns in software programming?

251: Why it's important to identify patterns?

252: What is Singleton Pattern and its importance in JavaScript?

253: How will you create singleton in JavaScript?

254: How will you create 2 equal objects in JavaScript?

255: What is the purpose of Factory pattern?

256: How will you create a Factory pattern?

257: Explain about Iterator pattern.

258: Explain about Decorator Pattern.

259: What is the importance of Strategy Pattern?

260: Explain data validation using strategy pattern.

261: Explain Façade pattern with example.

262: Explain about Proxy Pattern.

263: Explain about Mediator pattern.

264: Explain about Observer Pattern.

HR Questions

1: Tell me about a time when you worked additional hours to finish a project.

2: Tell me about a time when your performance exceeded the duties and requirements of your job.

3: What is your driving attitude about work?

4: Do you take work home with you?

5: Describe a typical work day to me.

6: Tell me about a time when you went out of your way at your previous job.

7: Are you open to receiving feedback and criticisms on your job performance, and adjusting as necessary?

8: What inspires you?

9: How do you inspire others?

10: What has been your biggest success?

11: What motivates you?

12: What do you do when you lose motivation?

13: What do you like to do in your free time?

14: What sets you apart from other workers?

15: Why are you the best candidate for that position?

16: What does it take to be successful?

17: What would be the biggest challenge in this position for you?

18: Would you describe yourself as an introvert or an extrovert?

19: What are some positive character traits that you don't possess?

20: What is the greatest lesson you've ever learned?

21: Have you ever been in a situation where one of your strengths became a weakness in an alternate setting?

22: Who has been the most influential person in your life?

23: Do you consider yourself to be a "detailed" or "big picture" type of person?

24: What is your greatest fear?

25: What sort of challenges do you enjoy?

26: Tell me about a time you were embarrassed. How did you handle it?

27: What is your greatest weakness?

28: What are the three best adjectives to describe you in a work setting?

29: What are the three best adjectives to describe you in your personal life?

30: What type of worker are you?

31: Tell me about your happiest day at work.

32: Tell me about your worst day at work.

33: What are you passionate about?

34: What is the piece of criticism you receive most often?

35: What type of work environment do you succeed the most in?

36: Are you an emotional person?

37: How do you make decisions?

38: What are the most difficult decisions for you to make?

39: When making a tough decision, how do you gather information?

40: Tell me about a decision you made that did not turn out well.

41: Are you able to make decisions quickly?

42: Tell me about your favorite book or newspaper.

43: If you could be rich or famous, which would you choose?

44: If you could trade places with anyone for a week, who would it be and why?

45: What would you say if I told you that just from glancing over your resume, I can already see three spelling mistakes?

46: Tell me about your worldview.

47: What is the biggest mistake someone could make in an interview?

48: If you won the $50m lottery, what would you do with the money?

49: Is there ever a time when honesty isn't appropriate in the workplace?

50: If you could travel anywhere in the world, where would it be?

51: What would I find in your refrigerator right now?

52: If you could play any sport professionally, what would it be and what aspect draws you to it?

53: Who were the presidential and vice-presidential candidates in the recent elections?

54: Explain X task in a few short sentences as you would to a second-grader.

55: If you could compare yourself to any animal, what would it be?

56: Who is your hero?

57: Who would play you in the movie about your life?

58: Name five people, alive or dead, that would be at your ideal dinner party.

59: What is customer service?

60: Tell me about a time when you went out of your way for a customer.

61: How do you gain confidence from customers?

62: Tell me about a time when a customer was upset or agitated – how did you handle the situation?

63: When can you make an exception for a customer?

64: What would you do in a situation where you were needed by both a customer and your boss?

65: What is the most important aspect of customer service?

66: Is it best to create low or high expectations for a customer?

67: Why would your skills be a good match with X objective of our company?

68: What do you think this job entails?

69: Is there anything else about the job or company you'd like to know?

70: Are you the best candidate for this position?

71: How did you prepare for this interview?

72: If you were hired here, what would you do on your first day?

73: Have you viewed our company's website?

74: How does X experience on your resume relate to this position?

75: Why do you want this position?

76: How is your background relevant to this position?

77: How do you feel about X mission of our company?

Some of the following titles might also be handy:

1. .NET Interview Questions You'll Most Likely Be Asked
2. 200 Interview Questions You'll Most Likely Be Asked
3. Access VBA Programming Interview Questions You'll Most Likely Be Asked
4. Adobe ColdFusion Interview Questions You'll Most Likely Be Asked
5. Advanced C++ Interview Questions You'll Most Likely Be Asked
6. Advanced Excel Interview Questions You'll Most Likely Be Asked
7. Advanced JAVA Interview Questions You'll Most Likely Be Asked
8. Advanced SAS Interview Questions You'll Most Likely Be Asked
9. AJAX Interview Questions You'll Most Likely Be Asked
10. Algorithms Interview Questions You'll Most Likely Be Asked
11. Android Development Interview Questions You'll Most Likely Be Asked
12. Ant & Maven Interview Questions You'll Most Likely Be Asked
13. Apache Web Server Interview Questions You'll Most Likely Be Asked
14. Artificial Intelligence Interview Questions You'll Most Likely Be Asked
15. ASP.NET Interview Questions You'll Most Likely Be Asked
16. Automated Software Testing Interview Questions You'll Most Likely Be Asked
17. Base SAS Interview Questions You'll Most Likely Be Asked
18. BEA WebLogic Server Interview Questions You'll Most Likely Be Asked
19. C & C++ Interview Questions You'll Most Likely Be Asked
20. C# Interview Questions You'll Most Likely Be Asked
21. CCNA Interview Questions You'll Most Likely Be Asked
22. Cloud Computing Interview Questions You'll Most Likely Be Asked
23. Computer Architecture Interview Questions You'll Most Likely Be Asked
24. Computer Networks Interview Questions You'll Most Likely Be Asked
25. Core JAVA Interview Questions You'll Most Likely Be Asked
26. Data Structures & Algorithms Interview Questions You'll Most Likely Be Asked
27. EJB 3.0 Interview Questions You'll Most Likely Be Asked
28. Entity Framework Interview Questions You'll Most Likely Be Asked
29. Fedora & RHEL Interview Questions You'll Most Likely Be Asked
30. Hadoop BIG DATA Interview Questions You'll Most Likely Be Asked
31. Hibernate, Spring & Struts Interview Questions You'll Most Likely Be Asked
32. HTML, XHTML and CSS Interview Questions You'll Most Likely Be Asked
33. HTML5 Interview Questions You'll Most Likely Be Asked
34. IBM WebSphere Application Server Interview Questions You'll Most Likely Be Asked
35. iOS SDK Interview Questions You'll Most Likely Be Asked
36. Java / J2EE Design Patterns Interview Questions You'll Most Likely Be Asked
37. Java / J2EE Interview Questions You'll Most Likely Be Asked
38. JavaScript Interview Questions You'll Most Likely Be Asked
39. JavaServer Faces Interview Questions You'll Most Likely Be Asked
40. JDBC Interview Questions You'll Most Likely Be Asked
41. jQuery Interview Questions You'll Most Likely Be Asked
42. JSP-Servlet Interview Questions You'll Most Likely Be Asked
43. JUnit Interview Questions You'll Most Likely Be Asked
44. Linux Interview Questions You'll Most Likely Be Asked
45. Linux System Administrator Interview Questions You'll Most Likely Be Asked
46. Mac OS X Lion Interview Questions You'll Most Likely Be Asked
47. Mac OS X Snow Leopard Interview Questions You'll Most Likely Be Asked
48. Microsoft Access Interview Questions You'll Most Likely Be Asked
49. Microsoft Powerpoint Interview Questions You'll Most Likely Be Asked
50. Microsoft Word Interview Questions You'll Most Likely Be Asked

For complete list visit

www.vibrantpublishers.com

Notes

Made in the USA
San Bernardino, CA
19 May 2018